EXPLORING NATURE'S UNCULTIVATED GARDEN

by
DEBORAH LEE

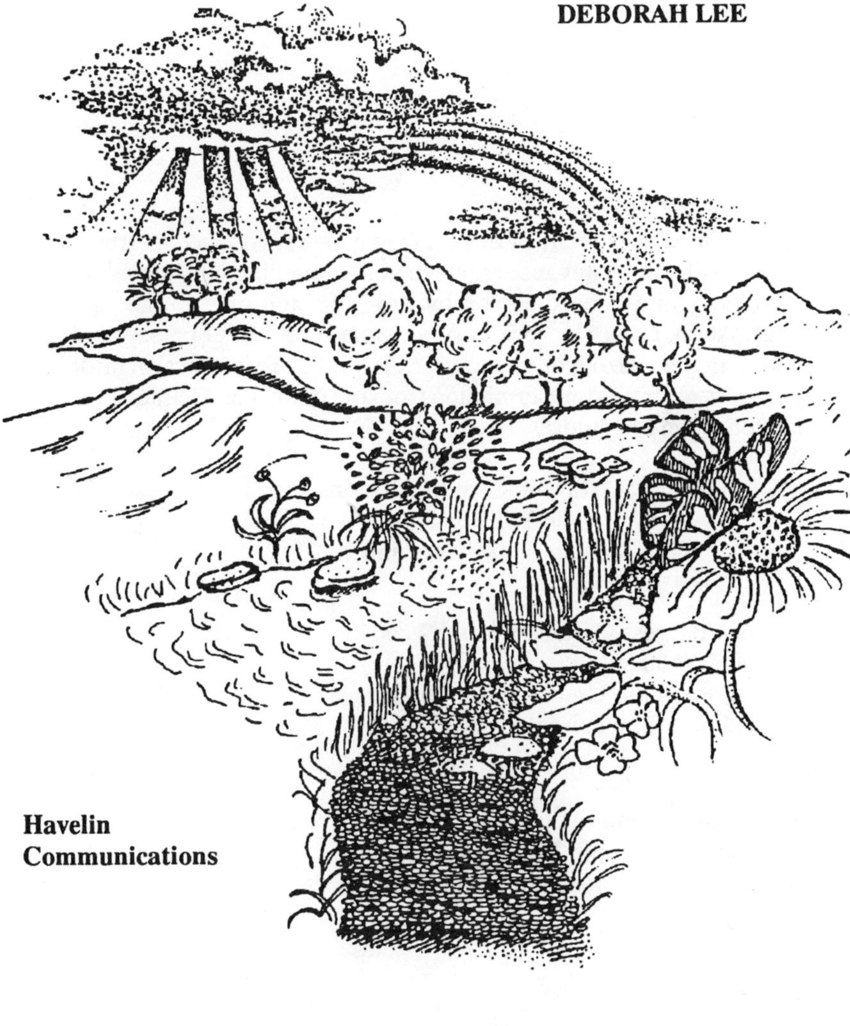

Havelin
Communications

Copyright © 1989 by Deborah Lee

All rights reserved. No part of this book may be reproduced or transmitted in any form by any means, electronic or mechanical, including photocopying and recording, or by any information storage and retrieval system, except by reviewers who may quote brief passages to be printed in a magazine or newspaper. Any other reproduction must be by express prior written permission from the publisher. Requests for permission should be addressed to:

Havelin Communications
PO Box 5630
Takoma Park, Maryland 20912

Library of Congress Card Number: 89-80046
ISBN 0-925909-00-9
Manufactured in the United States of America
Second Edition/First Printing

Cover design: Johanna Vogelsang
Front cover photograph: Michael F. Havelin
Back cover photograph: Nancy Smallacombe

ACKNOWLEDGEMENTS

Michael Havelin
For his precision editing, his coaching in punctuation and word-processing, his continuous support, and for his belief in this project and its author.
Thank you.

And a heartfelt thank you to the many others who freely gave of their time and expertise:

ILLUSTRATIONS
Michele Donnellan (primary artist)
Judy vonHandorf (supporting artist)

INFORMATION
Stephen Hoog
Anna Bond (recipes and proofing)
Luc Bodin (recipes)

TECHNICAL
Ann Jennings (first edition typing/layout and for the patience and support of a saint)
Susan Bradford (first edition editing)
Nancy Loving (recipe design)
Roseann Daveski (very first typing)
Loretta Jacobs (confidence to continue)
Elaine Thomas (proofing)
Steve Fogarty (Ventura expertise)
Elizabeth Riffe (general support)
Robert Onda (image scanning)
Shelly DePaul (first edition editing)
Maryann Brisk (proofing)
Maggie Martin (moral support)
Moyra Blank (proofing)

To Stephen Hoog

Whose expertise, wisdom, and macrobiotic insight formed the foundation on which this book was constructed.

PUBLISHER'S PREFACE

In the course of our lives we meet thousands of people. Most of them don't make much of an impression, some make a negative impression, and some leave our lives changed. For me, Deborah Lee is one of the latter. My life is different because she entered it and shared herself with me for a while.

I first met Deborah Lee at a nature writers' conference at the Pocono Environmental Education Center in eastern Pennsylvania. She had gone "knowing" that something significant would happen for her there. I had gone to hear what other nature writers had to say and to present my wildlife and nature photography for possible collaborative efforts. I had no idea that I would leave that conference headed down the road to becoming a publisher.

Deborah had been working as a naturalist and wild food expert for years, and was just finishing up an administrative position with the Macrobiotic Center of the Poconos. Because of her extensive knowledge in these different areas, she had been able to create a unique philosophical synthesis of natural foods and macrobiotics, and through her boundless energy (coupled with a special naivete which doesn't admit to obstacles), she had written and produced a workbook to accompany her wild food classes. That workbook was the first edition of *Exploring Nature's Uncultivated Garden*, written out longhand on yellow pads, typed several times professionally, photocopied and spiral-bound, and sold one at a time to individuals who came to her foraging weekends. She had just run out of copies and didn't have the resources for another printing. She was also sick of seeing the typos that leaped from the pages at her, and wanted to expand the book and give it a different look.

As we chatted, it became clear that this was an opportunity for us both. She needed a publisher and I was thinking of going in that direction anyway. She already had national distributors interested in the book. And there were other things we could become involved with too, including wild foods slide shows, videotapes and the like. We decided to go ahead with the project.

It rapidly became much more than merely a reprinting job. We decided to re-edit the text from beginning to end, and to change the book's size and format. We converted the original WordStar files to WordPerfect 4.2 format, a program which Deborah reluctantly started working with. After her initial edit, we went through each chapter again together in detail, using WordPerfect 5.0. Once the text was in proper shape and our designer, Michele Donnellan, had made certain decisions for us, the final layout was done using Ventura 2.0, a program I knew nothing about when we started. It has been a major learning experience for us both.

For someone who was absolutely computer-phobic when we met, Deborah has come a great distance, even to the point of sending files back and forth by modem. Her enthusiasm for the project never faltered, nor did my own belief in her unique vision and the importance of this project to a world facing an uncertain agricultural future. You hold the result in your hand. May it provide you with both intellectual and biological nutrition, and lead you along the path of health in the years to come.

Michael F. Havelin
Takoma Park, Maryland
December 30, 1988

INTRODUCTION

WEBSTER'S DICTIONARY: *Weed n. A plant growing wild that is useless, unpleasant in appearance, or harmful to cultivated plants.*

LEE'S PERSPECTIVE: *Weed n. A plant growing to restore balance in depleted soil, and/or to provide food or medicine. A precious gift. Beneficial to cultivated plants.*

Both definitions are correct; it hinges upon your attitude. This study guide was written to help readers appreciate the broader role of weeds in our environment, and how to observe, understand, and utilize them as a source of strong healing food.

My hope is that this book be a seed, stimulating readers toward a wholistic relationship with edible and traditional medicinal plants. The book is the next step beyond a wild food identification guide, written to get you down on your hands and knees to collect and scrutinize, then into the kitchen to experiment and utilize.

This seed is being sown at a time when large-scale agriculture is coming to its machinery-intensive, environment-disrupting climax. Agri-business is asking more from Nature than She can give. We must look to a regenerative approach to farming, working **with** the weeds rather than waging war against them. This guide offers one practical approach. Weeds can be managed through the three M's: mowing, mulching, and munching. I expound upon the latter.

My initial fascination with wild food was strictly romantic. It seemed like a fairy tale to dine upon dew-moistened violets or to drink dandelion-woodruff wine.

I studied wild foods as a child-like fantasy to complement studies in environmental education. My real task was to help clean up environmental pollution and destruction. At some point in attempting to tackle the overwhelming issue of where to start, I realized that it was impossible to clean up the external environment without first improving my own internal environment. Mine was in terrible shape, infections and continual pain were as commonplace to me as off-shore oil drilling is to Standard Oil. Step by step, I have experienced a steady healing of my body, mind, and spirit. With it has come the understanding that love is integral to the whole process. If we love and accept ourselves, we respect our body, and we keep it healthy and strong. Just so, when the body is loved and healthy, we appreciate and accept other people and the Earth - we keep the external environment clean as an extension of the respect that we feel for our personal environment. WE AND THE EARTH ARE ONE. When we heal ourselves, we heal the planet. I offer this book as one perspective toward cleansing ourselves and the environment, one bite at a time. Dietary choice is something over which we each wield tremendous leverage.

The book is divided into two parts. Part I: Theory, focuses on helping the reader develop observation and intuition skills that aim to build a foundation of knowledge on which to continually build. Part II: Practice, presents 75 natural food recipes designed to be healthy, tasty, relatively simple to prepare, and easy to modify according your imagination and foraging. Along with with the recipes are tips about seasonal plant characteristics. Approximately 140 plant species are discussed which are common to the temperate climate regions of the world.

Last summer I met a man and woman from India who run a Ayurvedic medical school in that country. They had come to the United States to examine our weeds. "You can tell what diseases are prevalent in an area," they said "by looking at the weeds which are abundant. The free-yielding plants will cure the illnesses of the people who live among them. Such is the ancient wisdom of India's Ayurvedic medicine."

Dandelion and plantain are abundant in cities and in people's yards. We discussed this. Dandelion is a general systemic restorative, strengthening the liver to cleanse toxins from the blood, thus enabling us to better cope in a polluted world. Plantain (both broad-leaf and lance-leaf) is an antiseptic and an antibiotic. Taken internally or applied externally, it fights infection and strengthens the lymphatic system. Can it be that the plantain is growing in such profusion to help with AIDS and other breakdowns of the lymphatic system?

There is much to learn from the weeds which surround us. Pesky enemies or benevolent providers - the perception is in the eye of the beholder.....your eye.

> Deborah Lee
> Huntly, Virginia
> January 3, 1989

TABLE of CONTENTS

PART I - THEORY 1

GETTING STARTED 3
    DEBORAH'S STORY 3
    HOW TO START 8
    PRECAUTIONS AND TIPS 10
    FINDING BALANCE 11

WHY WILD FOODS 13
    COMMON REASONS 14
    DEEPER REASONS 15
    WILD FOODS ARE SMALL BUT POTENT 17
    FIELD TO SHELF 19
    SOIL IS CRUCIAL 20
    HARMONY THROUGH ACTION 22
    BACKGROUND 25

DOCTRINES OF SIGNATURES AND SIMILARS 25
    MAKING USE 28

UNDERSTANDING BALANCE 29
    THE UNIFYING PRINCIPLE 29
    ENERGY INPLANTS 32
    RELATIVE TERMS 35
    GROWTH CHARACTERISTICS 35
    ENVIRONMENT AND SEASONAL CHANGE 45
    PREPARATION AND COOKING 47
    JUDGING SYSTEMIC CONDITION 49
    SUMMARY 50
    CLASSIFYING THREE EDIBLE PLANTS 51
    YIN-YANG CONTINUUM 55

FIVE TRANSFORMATIONS THEORY 57
    APPLYING THEORY TO PRACTICE 63

INTUITION EXERCISES 67
    VIBRATIONAL FIELDS 67
    OBSERVING 68
    GIVING THANKS 70
    BECOMING AWARE 71
    ATTENTIVENESS TO HOUSE PLANTS 72
    FEELING KI 73
    MUSCLE TEST 74
    TASTE TEST 76
    SUMMARY 77

PART II - PRACTICE

SEASONAL PLANTS AND THEIRUSES 81
    MAKING USE 81
    SIMPLE FOOD: A BLESSING 82
    140 SPECIES 83
    MODERATION, PLEASE 83
    REMEMBER 84
    FEEDBACK 85

SPRING FORAGING 87
    GREENS 89
    ROOTS AND TUBERS 98
    FLOWERS AND FRUIT 101
    MUSHROOMS 105

SUMMER FORAGING 109
    HERBS AND SPICES 110
    GENERAL MEDICINAL TEAS 114
    FRUITS AND BERRIES 117
    GREENS 121
    ROOTS AND TUBERS 125
    MUSHROOMS 127

LATE SUMMER FORAGING	129
AUTUMN FORAGING	133
ROOTS, TUBERS, RHIZOMES	134
GREENS	141
GRAINS	146
NUTS	150
FRUIT	154
WINTER FORAGING	161
GREENS	162
ROOTS AND TUBERS	166
FRUITS AND BERRIES	172
CONCLUSION	175
ENDNOTES	177
GLOSSARY	179
REFERENCES	181
INDEX OF COMMON NAMES AND GENERA	187
INDEX	189

TABLE of RECIPES

SPRING FORAGING

GREENS
- SPRING ROMANCE SALAD 92
- REDBUD SORREL SALAD 92
- SPRING PRESSED SALAD 93
- NETTLE POTAGE 93
- SPRING SAUTE 94
- NETTLE-TOFU CASSEROLE 95
- STUFFED GRAPE LEAVES 95
- SPRING TAMARI PICKLES 96
- KNOTWEED-APPLE PIE 97

ROOTS AND TUBERS
- COUNTRY WHEAT AND RYE 99
- YANG PANCAKES 100
- RAMP MISO 100

FLOWERS AND FRUIT
- ELDER BLOSSOM FRITTERS 102
- BERRY COMPOTE 104
- JUNEBERRY PARFAIT 104

MUSHROOMS
- WATERCRESS MUSHROOMS 106
- BARLEY-BEAN SOUP WITH MUSHROOMS 106

HERBS AND SPICES
- EVERYDAY BEVERAGE 113
- HERBAL RELAXANT 113

GENERAL MEDICINAL TEAS
- BAKED TROUT 115
- TABOULI 115
- SPICY OATMEAL CEREAL 116

FRUITS AND BERRIES
- BLUEBERRY PIE 119
- CHERRY-WALNUT CRUNCH 120
- CORNMEAL-WILD FRUIT MUFFINS 120
- COUSCOUS CAKE 121

GREENS
- CREAMY SORREL SOUP 122
- STEAMED VIOLET AND CABBAGE 123
- SUMMER SALAD 124
- SUKIYAKI 124

ROOTS AND TUBERS
- BEANS AND DANDELION ROOT 126
- MISO SOUP 127

MUSHROOMS

AUTUMN FORAGING

ROOTS, TUBERS, RHIZOMES
- NISHIME 136
- FRIED RICE 137
- BAKED PARSNIPS 138
- AUTUMN STEW 139
- BROWN RICE, BURDOCK, AND DRIED TOFU 140
- WHOLE WHEAT BERRIES AND WILD PARSNIP 140

GREENS
- CARROT TOP PESTO 142
- WILD GREENS SAUTE 143
- WATERCRESS, KALE, AND CABBAGE 144
- DANDELION ONION TEMPURA 144
- MILLET SOUP 145
- AUTUMN BOILED SALAD 146

GRAINS
- WILD RICE WITH HAZELNUTS AND BLUEBERRIES 148
- THANKSGIVING STUFFED SQUASH 148
- PORRIDGE 149
- WHOLE WHEAT BREAD 150

NUTS
- ACORN GRIDDLE CAKES 152
- BAKED RICE AND CHESTNUTS 152
- FLOURLESS NUT COOKIES 153
- WINTER SQUASH AND NUT DESSERT 154

FRUIT
- MEATLESS PEMMICAN 155
- APPLE-GRAPE COMPOTE 156
- PERSIMMON BUTTER 156
- FRUIT BARS 157
- WILD FRUIT SYRUP AND JELLY 157
- JERUSALEM ARTICHOKE-RAMP SAUTE 158
- JERUSALEM ARTICHOKE PICKLES 158

WINTER FORAGING

GREENS
- DRIED GREENS STOCK 163
- BARLEY PORRIDGE 164
- WINTERCRESS AND TAHINI 164
- STUFFED CABBAGE ROLLS 165
- WATERCRESS SUSHI 165

ROOTS AND TUBERS
- SOFT MILLET WITH WILD PARSNIP 167
- SWEET RICE, BURDOCK ROOT, AND SQUASH 167
- BUCKWHEAT PATTIES 168
- BURDOCK-CARROT KINPIRA 169
- BUCKWHEAT RAMEN WITH ROOTS 169
- COFFEE SUBSTITUTE 170

MOCHA PUDDING 171
GINGER FISH 171
FRUITS AND BERRIES
CRANBERRY SAUCE 173
ROSE HIP SYRUP 173
HOLIDAY PUNCH 174

PART I - THEORY

> Whether you and I and a few others will renew the world someday remains to be seen. But within ourselves we must renew it each day.
>
> *Herman Hesse.*

GETTING STARTED

DEBORAH'S STORY

Some of my most memorable childhood adventures took place when my father, grandfather and I went on spring mushroom hunts, enjoyed autumn fishing and persimmon trips, and explored the fields and woods of our Illinois farm. These were precious times for me, and when college began in 1968, I found myself wanting to spend most weekends and vacations camping, backpacking, hiking, and being outdoors.

After completing college, I led wilderness camping trips and regularly carried a 45-pound backpack. One hot day in Arizona, I sat down beside a stream with a cheese sandwich I'd carried twenty-six miles into a canyon. Before I started to eat, a fellow hiker exclaimed, "Look, watercress. Let's add it to our sandwiches." Dubiously I questioned, "Are you sure it's safe to eat?" My friend was already munching. Always ready for a new adventure, I tried some. It was tangy and a big improvement to my overly dry sandwich. At that moment I experienced a leap of consciousness and I began to wonder if masochistically carrying a heavy pack of Rice-a-Roni, Twinkies, and Colby cheese was entirely necessary. From that point I slowly began to expand on the small knowledge of wild foods I'd obtained from childhood.

In 1976, I started a masters program in Environmental Education. As part of the degree format, I designed a project to learn 100 wild foods and how to utilize them. After several months, I had catalogued eighty-eight edibles on our five acres of woods and meadow in eastern Kansas; the remaining twelve species were within easy walking distance. An abundance of free food was everywhere! This discovery challenged me to investigate further.

For years I studied every plant identification book within reach. I took community education classes on wild edibles. I followed old-timers through the woods. I studied with Native American teachers. Most of all, I experimented. One Kansas spring my roommate and I vowed to buy no vegetables from mid-February (when nettle, dock, and watercress began to grow) until our garden began to provide for us in mid to late May. We made nettle quiche and omelets, dock soup, watercress salads, and many other wonderful dishes (plus a couple of horrible concoctions). Cooking and eating the food took my study from an intellectual to a practical realm. It became easier to remember a plant after I had interacted with it by locating it, learning its season of edibility, collecting it, and then incorporating it into my style of eating. The learning became much simpler and very enjoyable. My reference books became worn and weathered friends.

I tried to memorize many facts about utilizing the 100-plus wild edibles and medicinal plants in my journal. I learned that kinnikinik is good for kidneys, dandelion greens act as a liver tonic and blood purifier, and rose hips are high in vitamin C. Yet it was extremely difficult to keep everything straight despite a shelf of reference books and pages of notes. How did native people remember all this? It seemed there had to be a simpler way - some kind of connecting factor or system. It was this question that drew me to the study of macrobiotics and new lessons on the edibility and use of plants.

Macrobiotic means: to take the bigger (macro) view of life (biotic). It is a wholistic perspective based on Japanese and Chinese observations of energy movement. I commenced to study a macrobiotic approach to food and healing in 1982 and gained an entirely new understanding of plant growth. Most remarkable was the insight that a plant could be looked at to determine whether it was edible or poisonous. It was so obvious. Why had I been blind to this before? This ancient system revealed medicinal uses as well as nutritional ones. The flood of wisdom humbled me and the thought surfaced that we consider ourselves advanced as a modern culture, yet we can't even look at a plant and know whether it will heal us or kill us.

Studying the ancient Oriental theory of balance (the Unifying Principle) and understanding the ancient Chinese Theory of Five Transformations helped me to see, as primitive people had, that similar patterns occurred in all living forms and in nature. The edible and medicinal uses of plants stood out as easy-to-observe threads of a perfectly woven tapestry. Warp and weft of the weave were the polar opposites of an energy pattern which flows through all life. I needed to study eastern theories on healing with food and herbs in order to observe wild edibles in a broader sense.

The age-old Oriental approaches are more empirical and wholistic than the Western scientific mode of thinking. Oriental herbal knowledge, for example, is based largely on observation, experience, and intuition, while western medicine focuses on experimenting, separating, and analyzing. To demonstrate this difference, consider the example of the common cold. Both schools of healing deem vitamin C a helpful remedy. However, in the macrobiotic viewpoint many other factors are also considered important.

Rose hips, the fruit of the wild rose, are extremely high in vitamin C. A scientific perspective will conclude that if a substance is high in vitamin C, then it is good for colds. This is a linear cause and effect relationship. The traditional outlook of eastern cultures is to see cycles and broad influences. Many aspects of the rose hip are observed. It is high in vitamin C, is found in temperate zones, matures in late summer, is red, quite small, and tart. The wholistic view will note that it stays on the vine all winter and is an important food source for birds and other animals. In addition, other foods high in vitamin C will also be considered: oranges which are large, sweet, juicy, and which grow in tropical or subtropical climates; and leafy greens including kale which has large, dark leaves and which thrives in temperate zones. According to Oriental medicine, each food is known to have an entirely different effect on the body. Seasonal and climatic conditions are also important. A person having a winter cold in Maine might be better off eating native rose hips or kale, whereas someone in Florida may be better suited eating oranges or drinking orange juice. This is because native foods, in the wholistic view, are seen to help the body adjust to climatic conditions. Oranges may be too extreme in their overall effect for the person living through a chilly winter in Maine and may actually cause the cold to linger. Oranges don't grow in Maine; rose hips do.

Both contain many other important characteristics besides vitamin C. Macrobiotic and Oriental healing arts view all these aspects as important.

The bigger view seemed a bit overwhelming until I began to comprehend the cyclical patterns of nature. Factors such as climate, color, and flavor are all essential puzzle pieces. Once I grasped this knowledge, the puzzle began to reveal its picture. With continued study of wild foods, I eagerly applied the ancient way of observing nature to my own style of looking, and started to understand that plant structure and habitat reveal WHY dandelion greens are a liver tonic and blood purifier. All the loose medicinal facts floating in my head began to fit into a pattern. Once I embraced the Oriental theories of plants, mankind, and nature, I realized that traditional Native Americans regarded vegetation and all of nature in a similar way. However, their approach is even more intuitive.

I had long before developed a kinship with the traditional ways of the Native Americans. So in order to get serious about learning from a close interaction with plants, I utilized an old Indian practice. I went on a vision quest and camped in the woods until an answer came. Using rituals I'd been taught, I asked the "Great Spirit" to show me a way to experience plants more meaningfully through direct interaction. The message came. Starting in a few weeks at the autumn equinox, I was to eat some wild food EVERY day and keep a journal of

UNCULTIVATED GARDEN

experiences, recipes, and uses. Even though autumn is an odd time to embark upon a project such as this, it proved to be an excellent method of focusing. I had moved to Pennsylvania earlier that year. This new foraging commitment caused me to become very aware of edibles in the Pocono Mountains region. I made it through the winter by collecting outdoors what few items grow all winter (primarily chives, watercress, and some roots such as burdock) and by relying on dried greens and roots collected earlier. The adventure went well. But when the first greens of late March (such as nettle, dock, day lily, and garlic mustard) majestically appeared, I was so thankful. It was a lot easier from then on.

The observation project has been a learning tool and a wonderful discipline. Many recipes from the resulting journal are included in the recipe section of this book. Utilizing some uncultivated food every day, I began to prepare each seasonal item in a variety of ways, becoming close friends with individual plants in the process. I saw many possibilities for each food. An example is a favorite friend: burdock root. Using small amounts at a time, I pressure-cooked it with rice, with barley, with wheat, with vegetables, and with grain and vegetables. I boiled it with millet, with corn, with rice, with barley, and made grain/vegetable stews. I used it in soups, sauteed it, water-sauteed it, baked it in casseroles, slow-simmered it with other roots and vegetables, cooked it in noodle dishes, and drank it as tea. Burdock root became as familiar to me as a domestic carrot.

From novice to weathered forager I developed an Native American model in which my learning came directly from the plants. I would eat a certain food on an empty stomach then observe its effects. How did I feel? Did my heart rate increase? Did my stomach feel relaxed? Did I feel suddenly connected to the web of nature and have new insights? Eventually intuition started to surface and propelled me into the realization that plants communicate quite directly if we have the ability to observe.

Through intellect and experience I've learned that plants communicate their use through their appearance, habitat, odor, taste, and other characteristics. They also communicate by an energy vibration that can be perceived by those sensitive enough. Ancient people, especially the medicine people, could sense the vibrations. Modern people can too; we just need to develop this latent sense.

Now, when I quiet my mind and stand before a plant I can become one with it. I can sense the water traveling up its roots and stems. I can perceive subtle vibrations in the energy field which surrounds it. If I quietly ask a question (such as if it's okay to collect this plant), an answer comes by way of a feeling deep within my intestinal center. Westerners call this trusting your gut feeling, or intuition. Traditional Orientals acknowledge the same type of response. They focus on sensations felt in the abdominal region, or hara, just below the naval. Eastern religions and theosophical orders speak of listening to the still voice of higher wisdom. Such communing is the ancient intuitive way of Seeing.

This form of sensory awareness stimulates the right hemisphere of our brain, which perceives whole patterns. The right side enables us to "feel" the world. The left hemisphere perceives the world in a linear mode. It tends to organize sensory input in the style of points on a line. The left brain functions logically and rationally. Using the tool of intellectual analysis, it helps us to "understand" the world. Ancient mystics and medicine people are likely to have been right-brain dominant. Scientists and intellectuals tend to be left-brain dominant. Faced with the challenge of healing ourselves and the Earth, it is time we all use our whole brains. When we utilize both intuition and intellect, an evolutionary process can occur. This is my reason for teaching wild foods the way I do in this book. I hope to activate ways of experiencing plants which utilize both parts of the brain: the sensual, picture-perceiving, right hemisphere being stimulated along with the fact-seeking, left hemisphere. By titillating both halves of the brain, we obtain a bigger view and the ability to see energy patterns. This expanded way of perceiving nature can help us feel unified again.

May the story of my experiences stimulate you to explore nature's uncultivated garden too.

HOW TO START

If you wish to forage, start with what is easily available. Often we stifle learning by limiting our options. We might say, "If only I could go to Utah and study with a medicine man," or, "If only I lived in the country." If you want to learn to forage, begin today with whatever meager resource is available. Start with something you already know. Dandelions and violet leaves are possible examples. Use them in numerous ways. Learn their seasonal variations, their flavor, their versatility in recipes. When you get bored with these species, try a few more. Persevere and more options will open.

As your interest develops, buy a good identification book. Several excellent resources are listed in the Reference Section at the end of this book. Choose a guide which has vivid pictures and concise information, one which allows you to carefully key out plants as to their characteristics and habitat. Eventually it will be fun to purchase, or borrow from the library, other foraging books which provide fascinating and informative stories.

A few tools can also be helpful: a pocket knife for cutting greens, twigs, stems, et cetera; a hand trowel for digging small roots or tubers; a garden shovel for digging large roots; several collecting bags or baskets for bringing produce home; and a pair of good hiking shoes that can withstand mud and tall weeds.

The most important tools to take, however, are your five senses and your intuition. It is crucial to learn how to slow down and keenly observe a plant. Pause to carefully identify the various growth characteristics. It is risky to eat something unless you are certain it is the plant you seek. Even then, polluted habitat may make it unsafe. That's when the still voice of common sense becomes your most valuable tool. Use it. Trust your gut feelings and look around for clues which support them.

Between a few good identification books and the information included in this study guide, a novice can go a long way toward supplementing his or her diet with wild greens, roots, fruit, and nuts. Realistically though, it is always helpful to study with someone who has foraged for many years. There's an old Oriental saying: "When the student is ready, the teacher appears." Just by experimenting and sharing the enthusiasm of something new, a student usually finds others who share common interests. The key is to take some direct action toward the goal of learning. Without this intent, you may not notice that a class is being offered.

Certain precautions are essential. Novice foragers often rush ahead and collect before they pause to see the entire picture. They may pick right beside a busy road or where weeds have been sprayed, mistake one species for another, needlessly pull plant and its root, pick an area clean, or gather part of plant (such as leaves) after its edible period. Please remember the following suggestions. They are simple, yet they can prevent many mistakes.

PRECAUTIONS AND TIPS

1. Know what you are picking. Be sure it is the plant you seek. Many edible plants have a poisonous look-alike. Once the edible plant has been definitely identified, take a tiny nibble, then wait for 30 minutes to observe any adverse reactions.

2. Be extremely careful when collecting mushrooms. A novice can easily make mistakes. Learn how to key out plants according to their features.

3. Know what part to pick. One part of a plant may be safe to eat and another part toxic. For example, elderberry blossoms and fruit are edible, but the leaves and branches are poisonous.

4. Just because wild animals can eat a plant does not mean humans can. Our digestive systems are much different. However, if wildlife is NOT eating a certain, tasty-looking morsel, take heed.

5. Avoid plants in commercially fertilized areas. Some plants such as lamb's quarters absorb toxic levels of nitrates from commercial fertilizer. Also avoid collecting under power lines, in unfamiliar weed lots or lawns, or beside farmers' fields. These areas may be sprayed with herbicides or defoliants to kill the weeds.

6. Avoid foraging close to main roadsides. Plants may be sprayed with toxic, weed control chemicals, and may be absorbing exhaust from cars.

7. Be grateful. Before picking or digging, pause for a moment to give thanks to the plant that is giving of itself to help you. You may be surprised at how pleasing this feels and how special the food seems later when you use it.

8. Collect with consciousness. As foragers, we have a responsibility to make the habitat in which we collect a little better for our being there. For example, if you collect dandelion leaves, select three or four from each plant and artistically prune.

9. Take only what you need. Be sure enough plants are left to replenish the supply. Leave some for wildlife. They cannot go to the supermarket.

10. Once the food is collected, clean and sort it. No cook wants a sink full of muddy dandelion greens mingled with grass blades and half an ant hill.

11. Practice moderation and avoid gorging yourself on wild edibles. They are powerful foods and your system may need to adjust. Eating them may cause the body to discharge various toxins or impurities. You want this beneficial cleansing to occur slowly.

12. Learn to blend wild produce into a meal. Many wild foods have very strong flavors. To simply boil, steam, or saute them by themselves may render a rather powerful taste. Chopping a cup of the young leaves and adding them to soup, steaming them with cabbage, or sauteing them with potatoes and onions mellows their flavor.

FINDING BALANCE

Through vision quests and foraging, I have been taught by the plants that we can find balance with nature. Our actions are influenced by the various foods that we digest. If we eat without regard for our bodily needs, our actions become chaotic and inharmonious. If we eat with awareness by picking, preparing, and eating uncultivated foods, we will deepen our understanding of the natural order, and we can therefore make decisions that are attuned to it. This book is to help the reader see the bigger picture by looking at the smaller details.

May you walk in balance softly upon the earth ever in awe of nature's harmony and perfection

WHY WILD FOODS

To most people, the idea of eating wild (uncultivated) food seems very strange, even threatening. This is odd when we consider our history. Humans have inhabited the earth for nearly **one million** years as hunters and gatherers, relying on the fruits and vegetables spontaneously provided by nature. Within the last 10,000 years or so our forbears began to domesticate wild plants and animals, but they continued to forage and hunt. It has only been since the Industrial Revolution (approximately 200 years) that Western societies have stopped foraging for much of their food and most of their medicine. This is a radical step indeed and has isolated us from an intimacy with our planet.

The isolation is but a moment in the calendar of time. In order to help you visualize this, I calculated the length of time our ancestors have been around as measured by the length of a yardstick. Thirty-six inches represents one million years. The last 200 years equals less than 1/128 of an inch! Seen from this perspective, the idea of not foraging is a radical move indeed.

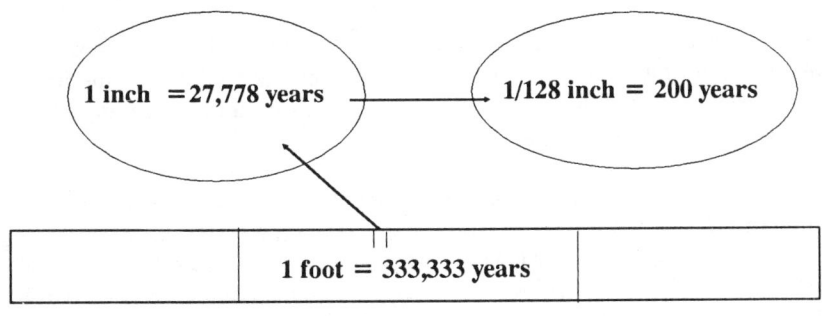

There are still a few people around who have learned foraging from their parents or relatives and who continue the habit. But these souls are rare in a country where ninety percent of Americans live the urban life. Our industrialized society is geared toward speed and convenience. Surveys reveal the average American spends less than 30 minutes a day on food preparation. Fast food and restaurant dining is a norm for most working families. It takes time to locate, gather, and prepare wild food. The average person simply does not have the time nor the inclination.

Foraging is not for the average person; it is for those of us who realize that our bodies are tools, tools that need to be kept in top working condition so that we can do the jobs we came to Earth to do. Foraging is for those who seek more than comfort and security. It appeals to the few of us who strive for health, clarity, and unity with the environment.

COMMON REASONS

When I ask students who attend my classes why they wish to learn about wild foods, they consistently offer several reasons:

RECREATION: To some, foraging provides an opportunity to be outdoors, to breathe fresh air, to hear natural sounds, to smell earthy aromas, and to break free of a standard routine.

CURIOSITY: Many are curious about vegetation. They want to know what plants are growing in their area and whether they are edible or medicinal. Backpackers desire to find fresh food along the trail rather than carrying a heavy load of supplies.

CONVENIENCE, FRESHNESS, AND FLAVOR: Some say convenience is a reason. To them, it is great to pick dinner greens in the yard instead of driving to the supermarket. Freshness is a factor here too. Freshly picked plants usually taste better, and they have a higher mineral and vitamin content than vegetables picked days or weeks before and shipped a long distance.

UNCULTIVATED GARDEN

COST: For those concerned about expenses, wild vegetables are free for the picking. The only cost is in the time it takes to harvest, clean, and prepare them.

SURVIVAL: In every class several students want to know what they can eat if they are stranded in the woods, or if provisions are scarce.

These are a few reasons why people feel the search for wild treasure is a rewarding and fulfilling adventure.

DEEPER REASONS

Other less obvious reasons to tap nature's bounty are also important.

SURVIVAL: We live within a complex structure of politics and economics. I marvel at how it keeps going. But it is a delicate, fallible structure. Parts of the system can easily break down due to strikes, oil embargoes, floods, droughts, transportation problems, military conflict, disease, and so on. We trust that food is readily available. However, we have polluted our environment so much that it is struggling to survive. We can no longer assume that weather patterns will support large agri-business. Or that a stable economy will prevail. It may become very important to know how to grow or forage for reliable sources of food. When we know what is available in the natural world, we have some control of our lives.

NUTRITION: Wild edibles usually contain higher levels of vitamins and minerals than cultivated produce. The following three examples provide some insight.

Let's look at vitamin A in leafy greens. Research shows the domestic spinach contains 8,100 International Units (I.U.) of vitamin A per 100 grams, while domestic swiss chard contains 6,500 units. This is a lot. These two greens rank among the highest sources for cultivated plants. However, naturally growing curly dock contains 12,900 units, lamb's quarter has 11,600, and dandelion greens have 14,000 units per 100 grams.

How about vitamin C? Domestic vegetables which rate the highest in C are green pepper with 128 mg per 100 grams, kale with 120 mg per 100 grams, arugula with 91 mg, parsley with 90 mg, and mustard greens with 70 mg. Oranges only contain about 50 mg. These figures are fairly high, but pokeweed shoots have 136 mg per 100 grams, curly dock has 119 mg, wild mustards average 118 mg, violet leaves have 210 mg, and rose hips contain a whopping 1,200 mg.

Calcium figures are interesting. When I mention calcium, most people immediately think of milk as the main provider. Cow's milk has 100-118 mg of calcium per 100 grams. In comparison, mustard greens contain 140-180 mg, soybean tofu has 120-130 mg, and sesame seeds offer a lofty 630-1,160 mg. Amongst wild foods, watercress has 90-130 mg, and lamb's quarter delivers 309 mg. The big figures come from wild seaweed. Kombu supplies 800 mg of calcium. Hiziki has 1,400 mg, and arame offers 1,700 mg of bone-building calcium per 100 grams. Knowledge of these figures helps us appreciate that we can get calcium directly from primary plant producers, and rely less on the meadow-devouring cows.[1]

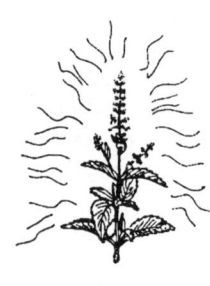

QUALITY: The quality of our food is crucial. There are some serious problems with quality today. We will examine why.

A macrobiotic precept is that all foods are charged with a vital life force. Some are more charged than others. Most ancient cultures, especially those which lived close to the land, were acutely aware of the life-force in plants. The Japanese refer to this life-force as ki; the Chinese call it chi; East Indians use the term prana; and Native Americans recognize a "spirit which moves within all things." The concept of life force is central in traditional Chinese and Japanese healing practices, and in this book.

The amount of life-sustaining energy in food is important because this ki nourishes the user. There are many factors in today's farming practices which drastically reduce ki: chemical fertilizers, herbicides, pesticides, growth hormones, and preservatives, to mention a few. Organic farming methods facilitate this natural charge, and within wild produce we find a tremendous amount of life-force. In a polluted world we need to obtain all the power we can from food in order to stay healthy. So ki, as well as nutrients, is of significant concern.

Most commercially grown vegetables, grains, and fruits are raised by a method called monoculture farming. In this system, one crop, such as corn or wheat, is raised in a field. The earth is plowed and seeds are planted. Herbicides and cultivation keep weeds away. Pesticides eliminate insects. In some cases, irrigation provides moisture. What remains are fields of finely manicured plants growing in soil which has very little biological activity. (Some systems even eliminate the soil and grow vegetables hydroponically in hot houses, using chemically-treated water.) Several recent manipulations include seed cloning which ensures that each plant in a field is identical to every other, making for uniform growth. Also used are artificial growth hormones, the effects of which include controlled harvesting whereby an entire orchard can be sprayed to ripen and drop its fruit at one time. We are drastically changing the way in which food grows. All these interventions interfere with the original form and content inherent in Nature-made plants, and with their ki.

WILD FOODS ARE SMALL BUT POTENT

Hybridizing of seeds also has an influence on life-force. Modern agriculture supports the creation of super plants grown from seeds which have been repeatedly hybridized: bred to resist drought, fungi, disease, and insects; altered to match a Madison Avenue concept of beauty; bio-engineered to be big and to look attractive on a store shelf for nigh on to infinity; and so it goes. When one trait is enhanced, however, several others often deteriorate in a process of natural compensation. Produce which looks nice may actually be quite low in vitamins, minerals, and ki. The archetypal configuration in which a species was originally formed has been altered many times over. Botanical hybridizing and genetic engineering appears effective, but we must question the results.

Plants from the hybrid seeds are, in turn, grown in a totally unnatural setting. There is nothing natural about monoculture farming. We may think it natural, or the best way, only if we are focusing on volume and efficiency instead of ki.

Our modern farms have become factories, maintained through the use of chemicals and machinery. They reflect a desire to produce maximum output quickly. In the short run, this is a very efficient and highly effective way to feed massive numbers of people. From a wholistic perspective, however, mass-scale farming produces many disturbing results.

Ironically, modern agri-business actually creates very weak plants. They are highly pampered and must be monitored continually. The plants have never had to struggle for a niche and become strong the way an uncultivated plant does. One act of nature can flatten a field. These plants stand as easy prey to a new strain of bacteria, insect invasion, drought, frost, hail storm, or high wind.

We eat these new-fangled plants and take on the characteristics that they embody. Our internal condition becomes such that we too, need a lot of pampering, such as thermostatically controlled environments, protection from

---

EXPERIMENT: In order to easily experience ki, go to the supermarket and buy several very large commercially-grown carrots. Then, go to a store that sells organic produce (or escape to the garden) and get several organic carrots. Finally, find a colony of wild carrots and dig three or four. The supermarket carrot may be a foot in length and two inches in diameter. By appearance it looks great, strong, and sturdy. The organic carrot may be half to one-fourth the size and may be a bit disfigured. It may look less appetizing. The wild carrot may be smaller than a half-used pencil and about half the diameter. It probably has root hairs growing out the sides and will be almost white in color. At first sight, it may look unworthy of being eaten. Now experiment. Cook with each, using them separately in a soup, stew, or other recipe. You may find, as I have, that even when you eat a large volume of the commercial carrots you'll still be hungry. About half to one-fourth the same quantity of organic carrot will probably fill you. And when the wild carrot is prepared in a dish, you may need only a small portion to feel full. Notice how you feel overall in relation to the food. You may likely feel calm and happy after eating the wild carrot (if you are a good cook, that is).

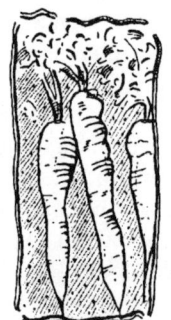

the elements, chemically derived vitamins, and chemical medications. Consequently, we can also easily be destroyed by natural responses of the environment such as a new strain of bacteria or virus.

FIELD TO SHELF

Once our food is grown and harvested, it may undergo mind-boggling manipulations to prepare it for sale. These also affect its vitality. Sulphites may be sprayed on fresh produce to reduce aging and thus sustain a longer shelf life. Artificial dyes may be added to make the fruits and vegetables look prettier. Flavor enhancers may be utilized to make fruit sweeter. Low oxygen environments may be built to control long-term storage (so that fall apples can be sold the following summer). Produce is refrigerated, shipped, sprayed, packaged and in recent cases possibly irradiated with nuclear byproducts to kill potential bacteria. I am talking about FRESH produce! Artificial processing of packaged foods can involve even more chemicals.

In our desire for attractive produce, no matter what the season or locale, we have tampered with nature to a shocking degree.

Our use and ingestion of chemicals and their effect on our bodies is profound. Some 400 billion pounds of synthetic chemicals are produced annually in the United States. Dr. Samuel S. Epstein, Professor of Occupational Medicine at the University of Illinois at Chicago, told the U.S. Congress in 1987 that most of these industrial chemicals have never been adequately tested for their toxic, carcinogenic, mutagenic or ecological effects. In addition, data from the chemical industry is, at best, suspect.[2]

Studies reveal that the average American consumes 5 to 6 aspirin-sized tablets a day of chemicals in food alone. The Environmental Protection Agency estimates that it allows at least 66 identified carcinogenic pesticides to be used on foods at the present time.[3] This means 66 bug killers KNOWN to cause cancer. What about weed killers and all the other toxins as well? Very few studies have been done on the long-term effects of toxic substances on the body, not to mention how the combination of thousands of these chemicals affect our bodies and our ki.

 It would be very easy at this time in history to point an accusing finger at big business, chemical companies, grocery store chains, and others. But the bottom line is that we caused this situation ourselves. As long as we, the consumers, demand or buy items such as tropical fruit in the winter, and produce which appears uniformly perfect, we have no right to complain. WE are the problem.

SOIL IS CRUCIAL

To further understand life-force in food, it is helpful to turn our attention to soil. When a field is initially (and repeatedly) plowed, the entire web of biological activity is disrupted. It took hundreds of years for soil to embody a biologically active matrix in which millions of living organisms interact to make nutrients more readily available. These interactions take place between fine root hairs, micro-organisms, minerals, water, decaying matter, earthworms, et cetera. Certain nutrients can actually be present in the soil, but if the conditions are not right, they remain unavailable to the plants. Left undisturbed, soil micro-organisms may actually transmute one compound to another to meet the plant's need.[4] Amazing? The key is biological activity. Plowing, cultivating, and spraying chemicals destroys most of this intricate tapestry. On chemically treated farms, and even on some organic farms, the soil is not active and the food's dynamic charge is often less than it could be. This is reflected in the vitality of those people or animals who eat the harvest. Most of us are unaware that modern agri-business is destroying the soil and poisoning our bodies.

Chemical fertilizers have been used extensively in this century in an attempt to replenish some of what is being lost in the soil. But farmers commonly return only three components: nitrogen, potassium, and phosphorous. Chemical attempts to artificially add nutrients are very incomplete, even though they have sufficed in the short term. That is not enough. Our soils are dangerously lacking in minerals.

UNCULTIVATED GARDEN

Organic farmers frequently revitalize soil with means such as "green manure" (growing buckwheat, rye, or other nitrogen-fixing vegetation over winter and then plowing it under in the spring). Also used are seaweed emulsions or natural fertilizers, including animal manure. These supplements are a very helpful step, returning what has been stolen from the soil. But the biological matrix is still disrupted when a field is dug up.

Left undisturbed, a dynamic electro-magnetic balance occurs between all of the plants. This happens above ground and in the soil. The strong survive because they can harmonize. They may even make chemical transmutations to do so. They are powerful sources of ki. Each plant is charged with a dynamic energy which transfers to the person who eats it.

A person who consistently uses some wild, uncultivated food (or produce grown by a natural agriculture[5]) may actually need to eat far less than otherwise. Wild plants are fortified with extra vitamins, minerals, and life-force; and when harvested in places that are not cultivated, they maintain an even mightier charge, and a harmonic connection to their niche.

The point is that when a plant struggles to find its niche and survives, it becomes strong. It adapts to change and hardships. These properties are in turn transferred to us.

Food which grows in dynamically balanced soil enhances our vitality, allows us to better harmonize with environmental conditions and with changes in general, and empowers us to re-establish our niche on Earth. Plant ki charges our ki.

In summary, I wish to emphasize that "super" plants which are grown in a monoculture and fortified with chemical fertilizers and pesticides are dangerously deficient. They are highly susceptible to disease, insects, or erratic weather. When a whole society is nourished by weak food, it is lacking in primal ki. It becomes susceptible to widespread disease from virus or bacteria. We see this in America where diseases such as herpes and AIDS are out of control.

Please realize that we can alter this situation. Each of us has tremendous power. We execute it each day with every dollar we spend and every mouthful we ingest. Let's make our choices consciously. If we as consumers demand organic food that is grown in biologically active soil, and if we carefully harvest the weeds, it is possible to dramatically change farming practices in this country, and in turn, to strengthen our populace. In order to survive and effectively heal our out-of-balance world, we must be personally healthy and vitalized with Nature's ki.

HARMONY THROUGH ACTION

By learning and using wild food or medicine, we harmonize with natural processes.

To successfully forage, we need to learn the habitat in which a species grows, its season of edibility, and how to prepare it afterward. All this allows for a lot of adventurous exploration, and provides sound reasons to get us outdoors.

The first thing is to identify plant species and families. To do so, we must get down on our hands and knees and observe. We look at colors and forms of flowers and fruit. We notice sizes, shapes, and textures of leaves. We perceive the height and breadth of plants, and we look at root growth. This can be a fascinating endeavor. As we practice identifying, we begin to understand what it is that we are eating, or not eating.

A trip to the forest, meadow, or marsh is somewhat like a journey into the unconscious, a tapping into the higher self. Each plant has its own particular needs, its own growing season, and its own habitat. Each plant sprouts, matures, flowers, and fruits in its own special time and place. As we study this sequence, each green gift becomes a new friend to which we must attune ourselves in order to enjoy the fruits of its existence. Step by step we learn more plants and their ways. The natural world begins to open up to us and the mysteries of nature reveal themselves. The unknown becomes the known, and we start to feel at home in natural habitats.

UNCULTIVATED GARDEN

We may traverse the same pathways season after season, during all sorts of weather and at various times of day. Searching these paths with identification books in hand, we no doubt ask the same questions asked by other foragers, biologists, old-timers, or ancient medicine people. Our knowledge evolves. Through observation and experimentation we locate favorite environments and most enjoyed treats. Finally, we develop the art of incorporating these morsels into our diet and lifestyle.

As we learn what foods we like and need, where to find them, in what season or time of the day to collect, how to gather them, and in what manner they can be utilized, we become a part of the seasonal cycle of growth and change. The "out there" doesn't seem strange and foreign any more. We may even find that we feel a lot happier and safer at a secluded stream than we feel in town. Gradually, we can experience a oneness and a knowledge that Mother Nature nurtures life and provides for all our needs.

At this point of our exploration we realize that we and the Earth are one. We see how vital it is to love and protect Her. As we do, we are then loving ourselves. Once we fully comprehend our inner connectedness with Mother Earth, we know our path is to become strong, healthy, loving, and deeply thankful for the richness of life. We see our own health and lifestyle as only a natural reflection of the Earth's health.

DOCTRINES OF SIGNATURES AND SIMILARS

BACKGROUND

Perhaps the oldest method of understanding plant usage was to observe it with a questioning mind. The term "Doctrine of Signatures" was coined in 16th century Europe to represent the knowledge that every plant has indicators, or signatures, which reveal its medicinal virtue or effect. The phrase "Doctrine of Similars" furthers the signature concept by showing that a plant resembles the organ, tissue, or condition of the organism upon which it acts.

For example, wild onion, garlic, and chives all have hollow leaves. Hollow leaves resemble the arteries they cleanse. The primitive plants of this family act as emulsifiers. They break down fats and allow the blood to flow better, thus easing stress on the heart and helping to lower blood pressure. Another example is lotus root which is similar in appearance to a lung both in size and shape, as well as internal design. In addition, it is mucilaginous. The root strengthens lungs by helping to remove mucus. These two examples reveal various ways in which signatures are offered by plants.

It is exciting to read signatures and indications of organ similarities. The task is accomplished by closely scrutinizing growth characteristics, plant function, habitat, chemical composition, and more. A few examples will help you get the idea.

DANDELION: Consider the common dandelion. Throughout the world, this little plant appears in areas where the natural system of balance has been disturbed. It is adaptable to just about any soil condition, and its toughness and tenacity make it one of the ten most "noxious" weeds. Modern man tends to fight the dandelion rather than understanding that it grows to help restore conditions necessary for a diverse community of organisms. Its adaptability is a signature which can be read to show the plant has numerous healing uses when ingested. One powerful use is to help restore internal balance. It does this in several ways: 1) dandelion works as a blood and liver tonic and cleanser by unblocking fat congestion and mucus build-up, 2) it stimulates the gall bladder and liver, thus increasing bile production and distribution, 3) it is a diuretic that increases secretion and expulsion of urine, thus helping the kidney to function effectively, and 4) it neutralizes acids and aids stomach action.

Chemical analysis shows dandelion greens to contain 14,000 I.U. of Vitamin A, 3.2 mg of iron, and 198 mg of calcium per 100 grams. All of these help build strong blood, bones, and teeth, as well as provide vitality. Bitter taste (discussed in later sections) stimulates heart and circulation. The mineral-rich root helps strengthen the intestines. Orientals considered roots in general to vitalize intestines because plants absorb nutrients through roots and humans absorb nutrients through the intestines.

Signatures for dandelion include hardiness, adaptability, and bitter taste.

BURDOCK: Burdock root is another prolific weed, also considered noxious due to its tendency to take over a field. It is a large, powerful plant with a sturdy, long root that grows deep into the earth. No little breeze will displace this mighty invader. It is apparent when looking at burdock that its power can help us become strong and centered. The long root speaks of its ability to strengthen

UNCULTIVATED GARDEN

the intestines it resembles. Oriental medicine indicates that blood is produced in the intestines. Burdock has an abundance of iron which makes it of special use as a blood purifier. Looking at the shape of the root can also give a clue as to why the Japanese used it as a sexual enhancer for men. The yang root strengthens sexual organs and helps bring general vitality. Burdock is utilized to promote kidney functions. It works to clear the blood of harmful acids. In this capacity, it is utilized for the treatment of arthritis, rheumatism, sciatica, and lumbago.

Signatures for burdock include power, versatility, and centeredness.

CATTAIL: The cattail is a water plant. Most land plants die when left standing in water for a week or two. Water plants thrive because they are able to regulate water flow. Their water habitat speaks of their ability to help the kidneys regulate fluid balance. (Watercress also falls into this category.) The plant's stalk is slippery. This characteristic indicates alkalinity, showing how cattail can alkalinize our blood when we've eaten too much red meat and sugary foods.

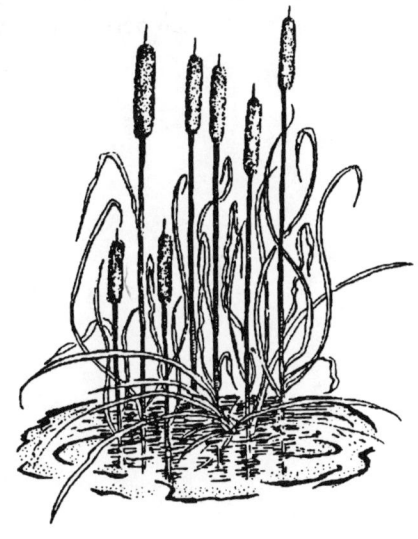

The primary signature for cattail is regulation of body fluids and pH.

MAKING USE

Reading signatures can be both a complex and a simple art. Like Sherlock Holmes applying his detective skills, we must observe with keen insight.

Let's experiment. Grab a few identification books, an herbal remedy guide, and a shovel. Go outside and find each of the three plants explained. Sit down by them one at a time, relax, and observe. Do you see the signatures mentioned? Do you notice any others? Once you have studied these species to your satisfaction, find three different species. Examine their features. What do they tell you? Look at size, color, shape, texture, aroma, and habitat. What uses do you think this plant has? Is it edible, medicinal, poisonous? Now open the books to check your observations. The task is simpler if several people are doing the looking together. Each person will likely notice something different.

UNDERSTANDING BALANCE

"Motion and change, and identity and rest, are the first and second secrets of nature: Motion and Rest."
--Ralph Waldo Emerson,
from his essay, Nature

THE UNIFYING PRINCIPLE

The next step beyond the Doctrines of Signatures and Similars is to explore why readable analogies exist between plants and humans. Plants are energy, just as we are. The same energy which creates and shapes plants also molds us, as well as everything else in the universe. When we understand how this happens, we have flexibility in using plants to create healthy lives. This sounds simple enough, and it is. But simple things often take a long time to perfect. So it may be with plant energetics. You can grasp the idea, then spend a lifetime observing it.

Religion and medicine of the Far East is based upon a thorough understanding of energetics. Ancients looked at their world and conceived that all things were a result of energy, or ki, which is continually flowing in a series of circular patterns that merge into an ever-evolving spiral. Within the pattern, energy flows from an expanded to a contracted state and back again, thus completing a circle and moving on to begin another. Ki changes from one extreme form to another, being never stationery. Ancients saw that all phenomena exhibited this archetype. They called this movement of energy the Unifying Principle. It can be illustrated as follows:

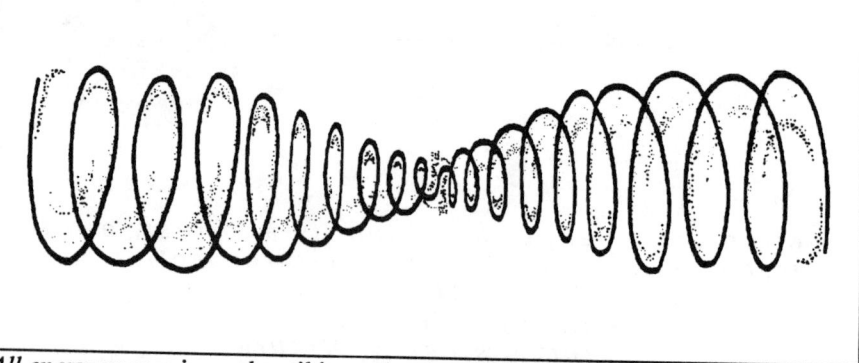

All energy moves inward until it reaches its most contracted state, then it changes direction and moves outward until it can expand no more.

To visualize the concept, it may help to think of water as an example. Ice represents water's contracted form. Eventually ice melts and evaporates into an gas which expands upward into the air. Cold temperatures at high altitudes cause the gas to contract into liquid and fall back upon the earth as rain, where it collects and eventually freezes again. Water never disappears, it merely changes from contracted to expanded to contracted...

The circular archetype is obvious in the cycle of a plant. A seed sprouts, grows, reproduces, dies, decays back into the earth, and fertilizes the seeds that it produced, enabling them to continue a new cycle of life. Another analogy is that of a day. Morning changes to noon, to evening, to night, and back to morning again.

The Unifying Principle is basic to macrobiotic thought. It states that two opposing primary forces (yang and yin) create polarity, and cause everything in the universe to come into being, develop, and eventually disintegrate. The understanding of how these universal forces operate intrigued Einstein and other physicists. It was, as well, a foundation for most major religions, including Christianity, Judaism, Taoism, and Buddhism, and Vedantic thought. According

UNCULTIVATED GARDEN 31

to macrobiotic concept, ANY situation, no matter how simple or complex, can be understood when viewed in terms of the universal law of cause and effect. George Ohsawa, Michio Kushi, and other macrobiotic associates have synthesized Far Eastern and other spiritual and philosophical modes of thought with modern western scientific and philosophical thinking in the book *Principles of the Order of the Universe*. (This work and others are listed in the Reference Section.)

Please note: Macrobiotic and Chinese theory are very similar, but the terminology is different. This is because after World War II, George Ohsawa simplified the usage of yin and yang in an effort to help the Western mind better grasp the concepts. If you are a student of Chinese medical sciences, you may wish to adjust these concepts to fit the more traditional understanding. I have presented the terms according to modern macrobiotic meaning.

In Japan, the term "Yo-Sei" was frequently used, meaning "yang nature." This depicts the contracting stage of ki. "In-Sei" or "yin nature" identifies the expanding stage. These terms in themselves show movement. Yang and yin refer to the two relative forces which shape the universe. In western science the word "centripetal" is used for a force moving toward the center, and "centrifugal" for a force which expands outward. In case your knowledge of physics is sketchy, centripetal (yang) energy can be observed if you watch water flow down the drain. It does so in a clockwise spiral (in the northern hemisphere that is; in the southern hemisphere it spins counter-clockwise). Either way, the water is influenced by a force which pushes it downward and in. The Japanese sometimes say Heaven's Force to help one visualize centripetal energy. The opposite force is centrifugal (yin). It can be observed if you drive your car at a high speed around a corner, or if you throw a tiny ball into a spinning roulette wheel. Passengers in a car and the ball on the table are spun outward by a force which the Japanese called Earth's Force.

Both East and West recognize the two opposing forces. However, to traditional far eastern thinking yin and yang nature are the basis of everyday conversation and perception. Western perception is much different. We in the West tend to emphasizes linear thinking as opposed to spiral movement. Western science is left brain dominant. It aims to separate, analyze, and look for causes and effects; it tends to look at either/or relationships. The eastern way, on the other hand, is right brain dominant: visual, intuitive, and conscious of patterns. To the eastern herbalist or philosopher, the forces of change continually dance, intertwining in all aspects of life.

The difference is obvious when we look at how illness is treated. In western allopathic medicine, a person is viewed as either well or sick. If ill, some outside force such as a virus or bacteria is seen to have caused the problem. The aim is to get rid of the cause. Many ways of doing so have come into fashion only to be dropped at a later time. Currently, chemical warfare is employed to attack the enemy: the disease agent. Take a cold for example. Germs caused it; antibiotics or other drugs are used to control it.

Oriental medicine looks at disease as an imbalance in the organism. The spiral view is that a cold may come every autumn and bring with it the opportunity to cleanse the body. The cold is not something terrible which needs to be immediately suppressed. A cold is neither health nor illness. It is the occasion for renewal. Since life is constantly moving and changing, each repetition of a cycle offers an opportunity for transformation and change. Herbal medicine uses nature's plants to re-balance a person's system. Western ways of healing come and go, but the plants never change. Herbalists use the same ones today that were used long before recorded history.

ENERGY IN PLANTS

In macrobiotic thinking several cycles in plants are seen to exist. Plants grow in a spiraling motion. In the northern hemisphere tops unfold clockwise and roots form counterclockwise. In the southern hemisphere the reverse occurs. Thus plant tops manifest yin (centrifugal energy) and roots have a predominance of yang (centripetal energy).

Yang energy is tight, dense, and constricted. Roots are formed by the steady flow of centripetal Heaven's Force moving inward. When we eat root vegetables, the formative energy which pushed them down into the ground also draws their ki down into our center where it strengthens organs which are deep and low, including the intestines and reproductive organs. This inward movement

UNCULTIVATED GARDEN

enables us to retain body heat. For this reason, root vegetables are good to eat in the winter, and they give us strength to recover when weak.

Yin energy is light and expanding. Stems, vines, leaves, flowers, and fruit are all manifestations of centrifugal Earth's Force flowing out. When we ingest the above-ground portions of a plant, the formative ki moves up and outward in our body, affecting higher organs such as the heart, lungs, and brain. These foods pull our heat out and are helpful in the spring, summer, and early autumn to cool us. Many influences are at work in above-ground growth. A diagram and explanation of the plant cycle will help explain the macrobiotic model.

When a seed sprouts, a polarity of forces causes two parts to grow: the dense, yang root and the less condensed, yin sprout. One is below; one is above. As the top develops, it expands upward and continually becomes more yin. This occurs as part of the cycle of growth and maturation. First to form is the stem or vine which supports the plant. From this, grow leaves. The leaves have a more expansive nature than the stem or vine. They are more yin. Flowers develop as the plant matures. This is the next stage of expansive movement. From flowers, come fruit. Fruit is the most yin, the most expanded, stage of a plant's cycle. At

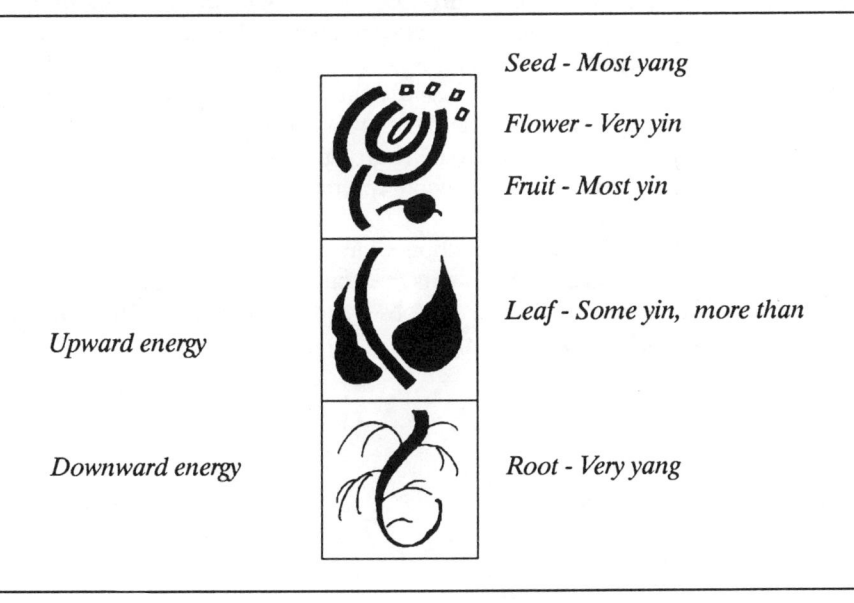

Upward energy

Downward energy

Seed - Most yang

Flower - Very yin

Fruit - Most yin

Leaf - Some yin, more than

Root - Very yang

this point, yin changes quickly to its opposite form of energy. Inside the fruit, seeds are formed. This seed (or nut, or grain) is the most compact stage. Within it is the entire essence of a new life. When it eventually sprouts, expansion occurs rapidly. A thrust of ki is generated at extreme transition points which keeps the cycle in perpetual motion. There is tremendous life-enhancing power in a plant. Ancient herbalists recognized the forces of polarity and cyclical movement and learned how to use the different parts of a plant to influence the body.

According to the macrobiotic view, leafy greens generally cleanse the liver and upper internal organs. Flowers and fruit affect the brain and central nervous system. Eating them will lighten the attitude and relax the organism, as well as stimulate the forebrain and generate the budding of new ideas. Neither however, provides the sturdy concentrated energy necessary to focus or feel firmly grounded. Seeds and roots fulfill that role. These functions are elaborated upon in the Five Transformations chapter, and in the seasonal introductions and subchapters in Part II.

The macrobiotic view of the movement of vegetal energy tells us a great deal as foragers. The serious student may also wish to delve into Chinese medicine, into Ayurvedic wisdom, and into the anthroposophic models presented by Rudolf Steiner. Each description of plant energetics offers a slightly different perspective. Analogous to this is the mapping of an area. One map may show topography, while another shows back roads, and a third shows major highways. Each map is different, but one is not right and the others wrong. Rather, each depicts a particular perspective. When a person thoroughly understands all the maps, they will have a good overview of the geographic situation.

We can apply expansion and contraction characteristics of plant growth and start to see the subtle effects which plants have on us when we eat them, be they wild or domestic. It becomes very easy to observe how the food we consume can restore our daily health or deplete it.

RELATIVE TERMS

It is important to realize that yin and yang are relative terms. Nothing is yin or yang by itself. A substance appears expanded only when compared to something else. For example, a flower is more yin than a root, also more yin than a leaf. But when compared to fruit, it is more yang. The flower by itself is neither yin nor yang. The same principle is true of its properties when ingested. This is why the Japanese speak of relative nature, be it yin or yang.

The ancient Taoist symbol of balance beautifully illustrates the Unifying Principle. It portrays how yin and yang energies rotate and alternate. In the diagram one side represents yin and shows that it contains within it a little bit of yang. The opposite side depicts yang, having within it a little yin. Everything contains a bit of its opposite and is constantly changing in the cyclical pattern from one pole to the other. At the extremes, one polarity changes to the opposite quite rapidly.

GROWTH CHARACTERISTICS

Once you have identified a plant, the following information helps you understand the subtle energetics at play and how these effect you. That's why this book is the next step beyond an identification guide. With it you can employ the Unifying Principle to features such as color, aroma, taste, and habitat. Many kinds of energy influence a foragable at any time so that a great deal more is occurring than mere maturation.

Within each plant there exist aspects of expansion and contraction. If there are too many indications of extreme expansion, a plant can be poisonous. It would likely act upon the brain and nervous system. For example, a poisonous mushroom is extremely yin. Eating it could cause hallucinations and other manifestions of brain damage. A herbaceous species which is dangerously expansive is water hemlock. Notorious as a poison, it causes paralysis, then death.

When you understand how to read energetics, you have the power of observation working for you. Water hemlock resembles wild carrot. The novice, and even the seasoned forager, can be fooled if they are not paying attention. The two specimens have many similarities, but water hemlock has purple markings which warn of danger. Most identification books mention water hemlock as a poisonous look-alike to carrot. Some elaborate on the differences. However, I find that many people do not take books along when they forage. Knowledge of extreme characteristics, such as the purple marks, may save you from making a terrible mistake.

GROWTH CHARACTERISTICS

GROWTH ASPECT	YIN (EXPANSION)	YANG (CONTRACTION)
Direction of growth	Vertical above ground, horizontal below	Horiz. above ground, vertical below
Growth rate	Faster	Slower
Size	Larger	Smaller
Height	Taller	Shorter
Leaf shape	Larger, rounded	Smaller, serrated
Light preference	Sun-loving	Shade-loving
Water content	Juicy, watery	Dry
Color	Flourescent, purple, blue	Red, orange, yellow
Aroma	Stronger	Little or none
Texture	Softer	Harder
Taste	Pungent, sour, sweet	Salty, bitter
Soil	Watery, rich, sedimentary	Dry, poor, volcanic
Environment	Warm, southern or tropical	Cold, northern, polar
Season	Grows more in spring & summer	Grows more in fall & winter

In addition to the extremes are numerous indications which can allow you to adjust your collecting and preparation so as to create a healthy balance with the seasonal changes and with your systemic needs. This applies to food or medicinal herbs.

A knowledgeable herbalist may employ an extreme plant for medicinal purposes, using it in small amounts. He or she does this because, when ill, a patient's system is imbalanced. Something extremely yin or yang may be needed to restore equilibrium before the body can heal itself. This is much different than foraging for general health. Your wild food consumption needs to be more centered on the yin/yang continuum. If a person eats too much wild food which is extremely yin or yang, such as the mildly toxic young pokeweed, it could throw their system out of balance. By learning the following signatures of extreme tendency, I hope you can develop internal wisdom and heighten your intuition. This will allow you to rely on your knowledge to enhance what is provided in various wild food books.

The chart below gives a few recognizable aspects of growth, or signatures, as to their degree of yin and yang nature according to modern macrobiotic classification.

DIRECTION OF GROWTH: Horizontal growth indicates contracting nature; vertical growth indicates expanding nature.

Plants which grow low to the ground (dandelion, plantain) and which have small leaves (chickweed, purslane) are more contracted than plants which display tall growth (pokeweed, Japanese knotweed, cattail) and have large leaves (burdock, skunk cabbage).

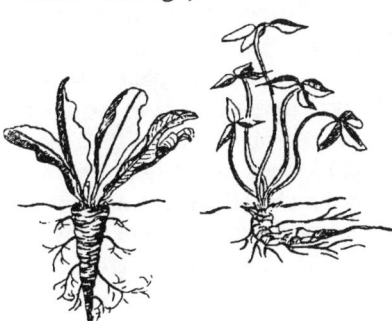

The same applies to root growth. Tubers (Jerusalem artichoke, domestic potato), or rhizomes (wild ginger, cattail) grow in a horizontal direction close to the surface. They are structurally more expanded than roots which are deep, vertical, and slender (burdock, parsnip, domestic or wild carrot).

OTHER FEATURES: Size, shape, water content, and need for sunlight are other signatures which can be relied upon to judge the expansive/contractive natures of a plant.

Let's look at leaf shape. Large, well-rounded leaves indicated yin expansion. Small, serrated, or sharply indented leaves indicate yang contraction.

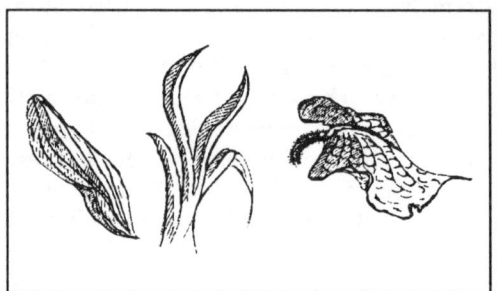 

Expanded leaf structure - yin.   *Contracted structure - yang*

Juicy, watery, and sun-loving plants manifest expansive yin;, while tough, dry, shade-loving plants manifest contractive yang.

The various signatures above show a definite pattern. A tall plant which has large well-rounded leaves, a large juicy stem, and which grows in a sunny spot manifests many expansive yin characteristics. The plant will create internal expansion when ingested. Pokeweed is an example. By the time this weed grows more than two or three feet tall, the foliage is poisonous to humans due to high levels of anhydrous oxalic acid. Growth characteristics are a clue to its extreme effect, as are its water content and color (detailed below). You can learn of pokeweed's toxicity by reading up on its chemical components, if you tend toward technical reading matter. Or you could simply look at the plant and see danger written all over it. I think that a realistic way to forage is to read the plant signatures and then do some research to back up your observations. You may be surprized to discover, as I was, that toxic compounds of many poisonous plants are still unknown. For one million years our relatives did not know chemistry, but the herbalists among them sure knew what to eat and what to avoid. Their information was gleaned from more than just trial, error, and word-of-mouth. They knew the language of plants.

A second extreme example is poison ivy. It is a tiny plant which grows close to the ground, has small leaves, is dry (as opposed to succulent), and prefers shade. All are contractive yang characteristics. In the spring, the young poison ivy leaves are red, which (as shown below) is also yang. The growth characteristics are just the beginning. But see, already these few tools tell you a great deal.

Now let's consider a non-extreme edible species. Dandelion grows close to the ground (yang), leaves are medium size but indented (yang), it prefers sun (yin), has somewhat dry leaves (yang), and the root is small, but vertical (yang). Overall, this hearty little plant is fairly yang and will give the user a lot of strength. Its structure is contractive, but no signs of extreme tendency are present.

COLOR: Color manifests along a yin/yang continuum in accordance with the rainbow spectrum. Red has a long wave length and represents yang; violet has a short wave length and represents yin. The other colors fall in between, as illustrated by the chart at the end of this chapter.

Color is probably the most useful tool for determining edibility. To use it, you must look at several factors: the color of the part to be eaten, and the color of OTHER parts of the plant. Red or purple are extreme colors if they appear on stems or leaves, giving a clue that the specimen may be outside the safety range for human consumption. When the stem or leaves of a plant show red or purple markings (streaks or dots), beware. Often the entire plant is either too constrictive or expansive to be edible. The coloration on stems and leaves also helps distinguish between friendly and poisonous look-alikes. For example, the poisonous water hemlock somewhat resembles wild carrot. Hemlock has purple dots on

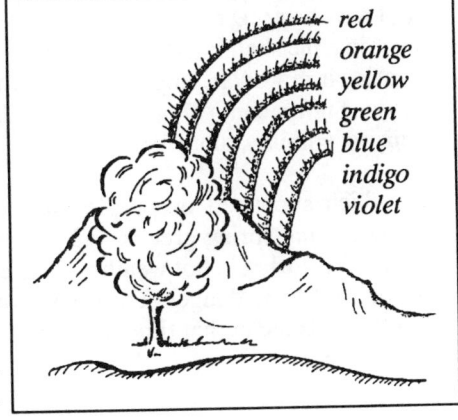

lock has purple dots on the stem. These warn of resnoid principles which cause the plant's toxicity. Pay attention to the purple! Without this knowledge a novice might mistake the poisonous hemlock for the delectable carrot. Milkweed and dogbane also resemble one another when the plants are very young. They may even grow side by side. Dogbane, however, has a red-purple color on its stem. It contains cardiac glycosides which make it poisonous to humans. I made the mistake of collecting it when I was first learning how to forage. Neither of my two identification books mentioned milkweed's resemblance to a toxic companion. I collected dogbane by mistake, brought it home, and boiled it in several cooking waters. The flavour was horrible, simply too intense to eat. Fortunately I had not ruined a casserole by combining the shoots with other ingredients. Now I look for extreme coloration, as well as several other identifiers, before I harvest milkweed.

Japanese knotweed provides another example. This rapidly-growing, sour-tasting bamboo relative is delectable when it first sprouts. Even then, purple color is splashed all over it. The new growth is deemed edible by many identification books, but caution is necessary. It exhibits many signs of extreme expansion. By the time the shoots are a week old, they can reach three feet in height and are toxic. Several summers ago a woman with a mild case of Multiple Sclerosis mentioned to me that she had a flair up of her illness after eating two of these shoots raw. Her systemic condition was very yin and the yin plant only made it worse. I talk about judging our condition a bit later, but the whole point of learning to read yin/yang features is to understand how to adapt our eating to our condition and to understand how to prepare our wild foods. Cooking adds heat and strength. Japanese knotweed is energetically altered by cooking it. In Part II, I have a spring recipe for knotweed which requires boiling it for an hour, baking it in a pie shell for 45 minutes, and serving it for dessert. This is a far cry from eating it raw on an empty stomach. Just because a book says something is edible does not mean YOU can safely indulge. The color clue is a big help in recognizing edibility, along with the other signatures explained in this book.

Plants which show red or purple on their leaves or stems are not always poisonous. Some spring greens, such as broad-leaf dock and dandelion, may develop red coloring in hot weather. This contractive tendency indicates bitter flavor, but not toxic danger. The color provides a helpful way to see that the taste is too extreme at that time to make it readily palatable.

UNCULTIVATED GARDEN

In addition to foliage, color can help with berries and fruit. Many purple berries are edible, yet purple berries on a plant with purple leaf or stem markings and expansive growth characteristics (pokeweed) are dangerous. Critters even avoid these. Red (or white) berries on a plant with red leaf or stem signs and yang growth characteristics may also be poisonous (baneberry, poison ivy). Within the known edible species, purple fruit (blackberries, blueberries, grapes) show a more yin nature than do red ones (strawberry, rose hips). Coloration on flowers indicates the same thing. Purple flowers (bergamot) speak of strong yin, whereas a yellow flower (dandelion) indicates less yin. Looking further, bergamot has a fragrant, expansive odor (more yin); dandelion has a fairly subdued aroma (less yin). Both flowers are about the same size, but the dandelion plant itself is more condensed (more yang). We can conclude that bergamot would have a more yin influence than dandelion.

Often it is difficult to discern red from purple or brown. In the beginning, realize that all these colors denote an extreme tendency. Observe this signature, then look at other characteristics in order to get a broader picture.

Fluorescence is a sign of very extreme yin and may indicate deadly poisonous properties. Some mushrooms are fluorescent. They may also show numerous other yin indications including soft or limp texture, and rapid growth. Avoid them.

AROMA: Strong aroma expands out and shows yin. Take skunk cabbage, for example. This wetland lover emits a strong, skunk-like odor when the leaves are bruised. The strong smell is an immediate indication that it is quite extreme. What's more, it grows rapidly, has big broad leaves, and prefers wet areas....yin, yin, yin, yin. This plant contains needle-like crystals of calcium oxalate and possible other toxins as well. Those who nibble its leaves never forget. When chewed, the crystals embed themselves in the membranes of the mouth and throat, causing intense burning and irritation. The root, though, is utilized medicinally.

Odor expands outward - yin

Aromatic herbs and spices have a great deal of expansive ki. One does not usually dine on a salad of peppermint or sage. You don't need to know yin and yang to figure that out. Their flavor is expansive as well. Aromatic herbs and spices are used in small amounts for seasoning, tea, or medicine. Their wafting fragrance is one signature of an extreme tendency.

Little or no aroma indicates yang. Flowers with little fragrance, such as violets, show yang nature when compared to other aromatic flowers such as marigolds.

TEXTURE: Texture is another signature. At one extreme are fibrous, tough, stringy, or thorny textures. These are indications of constriction: yang. Many edibles are tender and tasty when they are young (nettle, or thistle). As these mature, however, they become tough, stringy or thorny, and ghastly to eat. At the opposite pole are yin specimens: crumbly, soft, and limp. Stems which contain a great deal of water may be crisp or crunchy. Water is yin. The stem snaps easily and cooks down to almost nothing and imparts little strength or ki to the user. The same is true of a soft, limp plant or one which crumbles or collapses in your hand. There is very little life force to sustain the user. You will find yin texture in mushrooms. Plants in the palatable middle range show pith, firmness, and crispness.

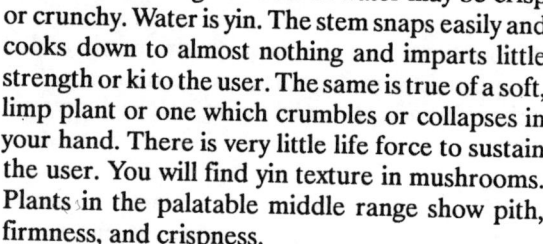

Thorny/yang; soft/yin.

In many cases we can assess a plant by feeling the texture. Some plants, such as young cattail, have a tough outer sheath which needs to be peeled back to reveal the soft and delicious inner core. Another example is plantain leaves. Young tender leaves are okay to eat; old tough ones on the same plant are stringy and unpalatable. In some cases you can pick tender, new top leaves when older, lower leaves on that same plant are inedible. Lamb's quarter is an example. Young greens are delicious in the early summer. Later on, this common weed gets tall and tough, but the tops can still be gathered and enjoyed.

UNCULTIVATED GARDEN

TASTE: Taste provides further insight into safe edibility. The chart below aligns tastes from yin to yang, beginning with bitter and ending with spicy. Japanese add "shibui" and "egui" at either end of the range. These terms are hard to define, but the examples in the chart provide a helpful hint. Both make you pucker and want to not swallow.

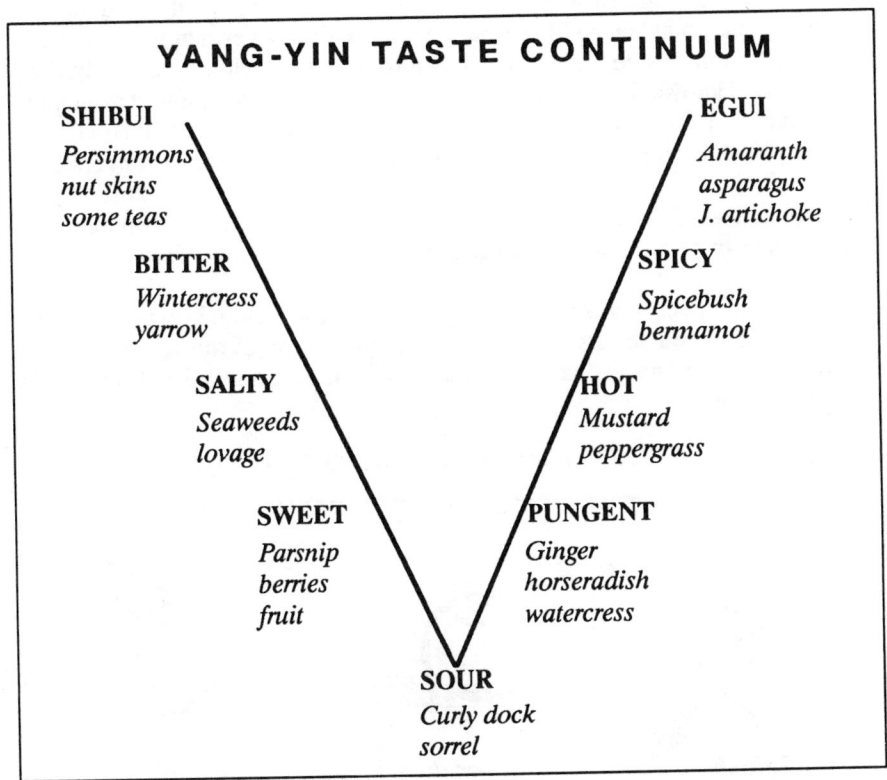

Tastes change each season, sometimes quite subtly. In spring, for example, the tender greens of many young plants taste sour. As herbaceous weeds mature and temperatures warm, their flavor generally becomes bitter. The plants get old and tough. After the first frost in autumn, a few herbaceous species grow leaves which taste either subtly sweet or pungent. I see this happen with dandelion, violet and others. The greens may not look much different, but their flavor has changed. The Five Transformation section explains seasonal taste variations.

Munching on unknown plants to determine their flavor is unwise. Identify the plant first. Once you know it is edible, then you can nibble and decide whether it tastes good enough to collect, and if so, how to prepare it for dinner. I emphasize this point because I see many enthusiastic novices sampling their way through the countryside. This can be dangerous. After a while, you may build a foundation of knowledge and the tasting habit can be based on sound principles and intuition. In most cases, poisonous foods taste terrible, BUT NOT ALWAYS. The water hemlock, for example, is highly toxic and its flavor is fine.

Taste, as indicated on the above chart, can be combined with other manifestations to determine a plant's overall expanding or contracting effects.

SOIL: Like humans, plants also have a preference for certain living conditions. They have favorite habitats and soil types. A discussion of this topic could be lengthy because many intricacies exist as to soil mechanisms.[6] The following is a brief synopsis.

Soil Conditions Affect Growth

Toxic chemicals.   Poor, dry soil.   Rich soil.

Soil conditions will affect plant growth patterns. A dandelion growing in poor, dry soil may have many different properties than one growing in rich moist soil. To the average forager, this consideration may be minor. It is more important when plants are used for medicinal purposes. Polluted or chemically treated soil is a terrible place to collect. Some clues can make these areas more recognizable. The chart at the end of the chapter illustrates soil types on a continuum from yin to yang.

When the soil smells odorless, silty, scorched, burned, or putrid, the odor indicates yang conditions. Plants which are able to grow in such soil need to be tough and therefore will manifest many yang characteristics. They may be too yang for human consumption. A versatile plant like dandelion might survive in highly unfavorable conditions. Pay attention to its signatures. Even though dandelion is edible, in this habitat, it might be too yang and probably too bitter to enjoy.

Strong chemical odor indicates yin (the aroma expands outward). A great many toxic chemicals could cause this odor, especially herbicides (weed killers). Weeds growing along roadsides, near farms, under power lines, in industrial areas, in urban areas, or on manicured lawns, may all be suspect. The plants and/or the soil can smell of chemicals. Either way they are probably poisonous due to extreme yin toxicity. Pick somewhere else. The conditions counteract the purpose of foraging in the first place.

Prime soil types include loam, humus, sweet-smelling, clay, and silt. Most foragable foods grow in these types of soils, though each fosters a different plant community.

The study of the weeds which grow in a given spot can be fascinating for gardeners or farmers because their presence tells a great deal about the soil condition, including whether various nutrients are missing. Many weeds serve the purpose in nature's grand scheme of helping to rebuild those areas.

ENVIRONMENT AND SEASONAL CHANGE

Uncultivated plants which grow in a particular region help the humans and wildlife which live there adjust to their climate. In a warm, moist, or tropical region, plants often manifest a great deal of upwardly expanding yin growth.

This feature has developed in response to the environment. Under such conditions, vegetation on a whole grows quickly, has large expanded leaves, and produces large and juicy fruit. Roots, on the other hand, may not need to grow deep for water and nutrients. Under lush growing conditions, roots tend to be small, often growing close to the surface because water is ample. These growth characteristics are yin.

In a temperate climate, vegetation looks entirely different. Trees and plants show much yang nature. Leaves tend to be small, serrated, or narrow. Roots may need to grow long and deep in search of moisture and to survive a cold winter when the tops go dormant. Wild fruits and berries are also small.

Similar traits develop in a hot, dry area such as a prairie or desert. In a prairie or meadow habitat, leaves are long and slender, a feature which prevents excessive water loss through evaporation from leaf pores. In the desert, cactus has spines instead of leaves as an adaptation to water conservation. Sunlight is readily available to prairie and dessert plants and they need not develop wide leaves to capture sunshine for photosynthesis of light into food.

Foods which grow in a particular climate enable the organisms living there to acclimatize to the weather. Yin tropical fruits (pineapple, banana, mango, and grapefruit) are sweet and large. These cool the body and help organisms feel comfortable in the heat. On the other hand, yang temperate climate wild fruit (cranberry, blueberries, blackberries, sumac berries, and rose hips) are small, dense, and not particularly succulent. Generally speaking, these warm the body. When we eat produce which naturally grows in our region, we find a comfortable balance with the climate.

Seasonal adaptations also occur, and we see this readily in a four season region. During autumn and winter, life force settles into roots and tubers, preserving and nourishing biennial and perennial plants through winter. Autumn is the best season to harvest these foodstuffs. Nuts, seeds, and grains also ripen in autumn, being yang and heat-producing. In cold climate winters, the few hardy stalwarts which thrive have small or serrated leaves and generally grow close to the ground, all are yang indications which enable the plants to adapt. Evergreen trees have needles which help them survive in cold, harsh conditions. Winter's edible weeds and needles are extremely nutritious and strengthening. In spring, young, leafy plant tops exhibit strong upward yin grwth. Eating them helps the organism dispel winter fat and adjust to gradual warming trends. The flowers, fruits, and mushrooms which come out in warm weather further help to cool the body. (Seasonal growing trends and their significance to the body are detailed in Part II at the beginning of each seasonal recipe section.)

PREPARATION AND COOKING

Ultimately, many of the foods which are harvested have to be prepared in some way. The transformation of nature's bounty into healing dishes is an art which involves energy. The chart at the end of this chapter shows styles of preparation ranging from yang to yin as follows: pickle, tempura (when served with a salty dipping sauce), bake, pressure-cook, saute, boil, steam, press, and raw. The elements of heat, salt, pressure, time, and less moisture are all more condensing or yangizing. Raw, light cooking, or watery preparations are more expanding or yinizing.

When we couple knowledge and keen awareness of collecting food with the art of preparation, we can control our health and interact with nature in an exciting way. For example, succulent spring leaves show considerable yin. If you were to eat them raw you would get an entirely different effect than if you prepared them in a very yang manner like pickling. What difference do you think might occur within your body? Please think for a moment. If you say the raw greens would relax and cool, and the pickled greens would be more energizing, you understand.

Let's look at another example. Suppose the yang burdock root is dug in summer and tempuraed, baked, or pressure-cooked. What would you expect the effect to be? It would likely make you hot, possibly even angry or aggressive. Soon after eating it, you might naturally crave something very yin, such as a rich dessert or beer to expand the contraction brought on. Now suppose you dug this root on a cold day in autumn, just before the ground froze, and prepared it the same way. What would happen? The dish would more likely give you much warmth and energy. The effect would be entirely different than in the summer.

This information is basically all common sense. Unfortunately, many of us have taken to living in cities, shopping in the supermarket, and forgetting a lot of what we should naturally know. We have to re-learn, and it helps to analyze food and cooking a bit in order to re-develop our intuition.

In the cool weeks of early spring, many foods such as mushrooms, sour-tasting greens, edible ferns, and certain flower heads combine several yin factors. If a person is not eating yang meat and animal products, it is wise to yangize foraged vegetables through tempura, baking, or other yang preparations. In summer, many wild items are delicious raw. They are quite potent because their innate life force body is not reduced by cooking. Eating some raw foods makes the average person feels charged, yet cooled. Salads, raw or lightly cooked, are great in summer. Other summer preparations include light steaming or boiling to relax the system, and some saute or pressure-cooking to invigorate. Summer is also a fine time for fruity desserts. In autumn and winter, our style of cooking must be quite different than in spring and summer. We want to eat foods which warm us, preparing them to further enhance this effect. Roots, nuts, seeds, grains, and sturdy greens come into harvest in autumn. By winter, it is wise to prepare them using yang methods: saute, pressure-cook, bake, tempura, and pickle. During cold weather we may still eat some things raw or lightly cooked, but not as many.

If you live in town and keep the thermostat at 75 degrees all winter or run the air conditioner at 75 degrees all summer, you are not part of the natural temperate climate flow. And your diet is likely to be about the same all year too. You are trapped. Why not break into a more natural process? Change your food and cooking styles and watch what happens. Any predictions? I have a few. First of all, you will be able to turn your thermostat down lower in winter and still be comfortable. You will stop shivering on those quick winter sprints between the house and the car. You will feel warm and more comfortable outside in the cold and may decide to take up cross-country skiing over racquetball. Same with summer. Instead of feeling hot and sticky, you will likely be bothered far less by 95 degree temperatures and may not even need the air conditioner. You may take to hiking or biking on a hot day rather than gorging on ice cream in front of a fan.

But don't take my word on these matters. Find out for yourself. That way you will really understand.

JUDGING SYSTEMIC CONDITION

There is one more important matter, that of individual condition. In this chapter I have elaborated on how to look at a plant and judge its energetic effect, then how to prepare it to further enhance or alter this influence. It is important to realize, however, that every person's systemic condition is unique. Foods will therefore influence each person somewhat differently. The next step is to apply yin and yang nature to individual condition.

We've discussed the fact that burdock and other roots are good for the intestines and blood. But each person needs to ask, "Is it good for MY intestines?" Your condition may currently be too yang.

YIN NATURE: A person who shows yin signs may feel weak, be unable to cope effectively or take on life's challenges. This person is usually late for everything, disorganized, indecisive, and has a messy house or desk. Many vegetarians and raw food advocates gradually develop these traits. Typical foods which generate this condition include: sugar, imitation sweeteners, honey, carbonated beverages, imitation fruit drinks, tropical fruit and fruit juice (especially when consumed in cold weather), candy, yeast breads, pastries (such as cookies, cake, donuts), alcoholic beverages including beer and wine, coffee, black or green tea, many commercial herbal tea blends, ice cream or soy ice cream, yogurt, milk, nut butters and oily nuts, many prescription drugs, recreational or illicit drugs and narcotics, and chemical food additives. These foods are considered yin. They tend to expand the nervous system. When a person has a yin condition due to the ingestion of these items, they can benefit from the preparation of strong yang foods coupled with yang cooking styles. Consuming more expansive foods would only add to the imbalance.

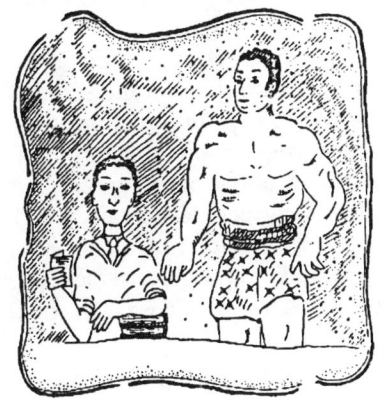

If someone with these tendencies harvests extremely yin foods such as pokeweed or Japanese knotweed, even mint, it might be too much for their system and could cause a yin reaction such as: rash, vomiting, difficulty concentrating, hallucinations, excited behavior, rapid heart beat, et cetera.

YANG NATURE: Conversely, a person who shows yang traits may feel overly aggressive, be often angry, tight and constricted, and may be very active. This person is usually on time for engagements, is very organized, makes decisions quickly, has a tidy, well organized house or work space, and may be intolerant of people who are less focused than themselves. This condition is likely facilitated by frequent use of salt, tamari, red meat (including pork, beef, lamb, organ meats and wild game), shellfish, eggs, fried foods, hard salty cheese (cheddar), crackers and chips, toasts, pickles, et cetera. To balance this kind of situation, mildly yin foods served lightly cooked or raw, may relax and loosen this condition. Various wild aromatic teas, spices, leafy greens, flowers and fruit may also be beneficial to restore equilibrium. But a very yang food such as burdock or ginsing, long-cooked, is not the ticket.

SUMMARY

We have explored many facets of plant growth, and each is an important clue to nature's cycles. We can now use this information for our health.

The next charts classify three edible plants. I suggest you locate at least one of these species in the wild and scrutinize the features mentioned. Then make your our chart to key out signatures according to yin and yang nature. With a little practice, you can soon sum up the energetics at a glance. At that point perceiving balance becomes second nature. It is like learning to play a musical instrument. At first many technical details must be remembered. Eventually the music flows and the lessons of rote memory give way to a oneness with the sound. By understanding energy movement in plants and ourselves, we can harmonize with nature by determining what to collect, when, and how to utilize it.

CLASSIFYING THREE EDIBLE PLANTS

BURDOCK   ENERGETICS

1. **Climate zone:** found in most climates	yang
2. **Speed of growth:** grows slowly, two years	yang
3. **Shape of leaf:** large (with scalloped leaves) - some yang	yin
4. **Season:** all seasons	yang
5. **Light preference:** best in sun (will grow in shade)	yin
6. **Water content:** dry, especially the root	yang
7. **Soil conditions:** wide variety, likes poor, rocky soil	yang
8. **Direction of growth:** strong upward and downward	yang
9. **Color:** Purple on stalk and older leaves	yin
10. **Aroma:** mild aroma	yang
11. **Taste:** bitter (with some sweet) - somewhat balanced	yang

COMMENTS: Root is very yang, leaves yin.

1. Use in moderation; excellent in winter in larger amounts.
2. Root energy is kept in the center of body.
3. Root contracts intestines, tonifies, a general blood tonic.
4. Root good for yin condition, for people with arthritis, for anyone with expanded heart and/or intestines, anyone having eaten large quantities of sugar or drugs, or anyone who has received radiation.
5. Leaves better cooked, okay for yang condition.

NOTES:

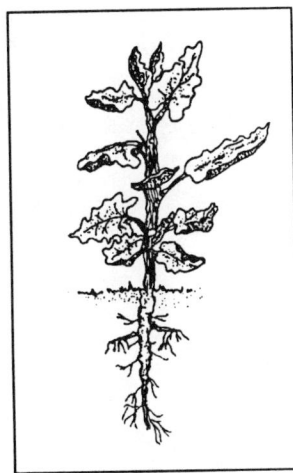

PURSLANE	ENERGETICS
1. **Climate zone:** found in most temperate climates	yang
2. **Speed of growth:** rapid	yin
3. **Shape of leaf:** small, compact	yang
4. **Season:** summer to early fall	yin
5. **Light preference:** prefers sun	yin
6. **Water content:** succulent	yin
7. **Soil conditions:** cultivated soil, gardens	yin
8. **Direction of growth:** horizontal	yang
9. **Aroma:** none	yang
10. **Taste:** strongly sour	yin

COMMENTS: Some strong yin and yang qualities.

1. Use in moderate amounts, all summer.
2. Sour taste cleanses liver.
3. Cooling - helps body move heat to the periphery.
4. To be used with caution by people with yin condition; for others, use two or three times a week in moderate quantities when purslane is in season.

NOTES:

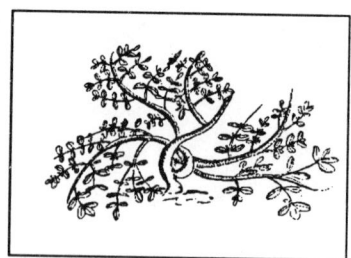

UNCULTIVATED GARDEN 53

JAPANESE KNOTWEED   ENERGETICS

1. **Climate zone:** cool, moist areas — yin
2. **Speed of growth:** very rapid in spring — yin
3. **Shape of leaf:** large — yin
4. **Light preference:** sunny (some shade) - some yin — yang
5. **Water content:** succulent — yin
6. **Soil condition:** rich, wetlands, beside rivers — yin
7. **Direction of growth:** strong vertical above & below — yin
8. **Color:** lots of purple — yin
9. **Aroma:** some aroma — yin
10. **Taste:** strong sour — yin

COMMENTS: Strong yin; use in small amounts, early spring only.

1. Use young shoot ONLY, before three feet high. Poisonous when mature - too yin.
2. Sour taste cleanses liver.
3. Cooling - helps body move heat to the periphery.
4. The strong yin signatures caution use in small amounts. Nibble a little, preferably serve well-cooked. Good for yang condition and liver stagnation caused by animal fat and oil. Better avoided by people with yin condition; can over-accelerate the system.

NOTES:

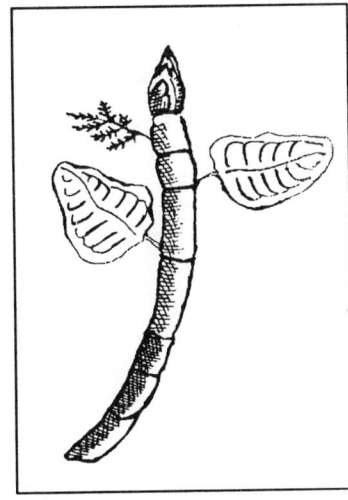

Construct YOUR OWN CHART below

PLANT: ENERGETICS

1. Climate zone:
2. Speed of growth:
3. Shape of leaf:
4. Light preference:
5. Water content:
6. Soil condition:
7. Direction of growth:
8. Color:
9. Aroma:
10. Taste:

COMMENTS:

NOTES:

Sketch plant here.

YIN-YANG CONTINUUM

YANG   **YIN**

    More Contractive Force   More Expansive Force

PLANT PART

Seed...Root.....Contracted stalk....Vine...Rhizome...Tuber...Leaf....Flower....Fruit

COLOR

Red.......Orange.......Yellow.......Brown........Green.......Blue........Indigo........Purple

TEXTURE

Fibrous...Tough...Prickly...Pithy...Firm...Crisp..Flexible..Soft...Crunchy..Crumbly

TASTE

Shibui.......Bitter.......Salty.......Sweet......Sour......Pungent......Hot......Spicy......Egui

SOILS

Alkaline.....Brackish ....Sandy..... Loam....Humus.....Sweet.....Silt.....Clay.....Acid

No odor....Scorched....Putrid....Fragrant.....Rancid....Oily....Rotten....Strong odor

COOKING STYLE

Tempura.....Bake....Pressure cook....Saute...Boil...Steam...Blanch...Pressed...Raw

PICKLES

Miso..................Salt bran..................Brine..................Relish................Quick salt

FIVE TRANSFORMATIONS THEORY

The Five Transformations concept (sometimes called Five Elements) is considered to be Chinese in origin. It is more than 4,000 years old, although based on common sense ideas much older than that. The theory was first detailed in the Nei Ching, an ancient medical guide written long before the time of Christ. Since that time the Five Transformations has been central to Oriental medicine. It still exists today because of its simplicity and clarity.

This theory illustrates the movement of ki from a very condensed yang state to a very dispersed yin state. Ki can take the form of tight, compact energy like a rock or a piece of metal, or it can take the form of light, dispersed energy like air or vibration. The Five Transformations Theory portrays a pattern of change through five phases. Its teachings can be an excellent tool for understanding the plant kingdom, as well as many other aspects of life. The theory is not a science, but rather a means of developing our intuition and wholistic thinking.

We may never know for certain how the Chinese developed this theory. The most obvious explanation is that the principles became clear as intuitive people observed their world.

To explain it to you, I feel a good place to begin is with the seasons. Each season has its own distinctive characteristics, its own atmospheric quality, and its own weather patterns. Spring, for example, is a time of upward rising energy, of sprouting, of enthusiasm, of birthing new ideas. This subtly changes into summer, which is highly charged with activity. Summer brings dispersed thoughts and action. It is a time of letting go, of play. Late in summer there comes a period of transition and downward energy. This stage is a time of increased mental and intellectual development, a time for assessing the summer's activities, and for education. It is a season of maturation and harvest. Soon afterwards, the energy of autumn gathers. This season is the closing down, the storage of the harvest, the preparation for winter's cold, the dying of leaves and other vegetation, and the end of a dream that began long ago in the cycle. Finally, the cold and barren winter allows everyone the opportunity to reflect on the year gone by, to draw on the reserves collected, and to tentatively plan for the year ahead. It is a floating time between past and future. Winter's cold weather encourages staying indoors, huddling around the fire, and thinking about spring when things can sprout anew.

Each season is distinct, yet there is no sharp break between them. Their cycle of movement is illustrated in the Nei Ching as follows:

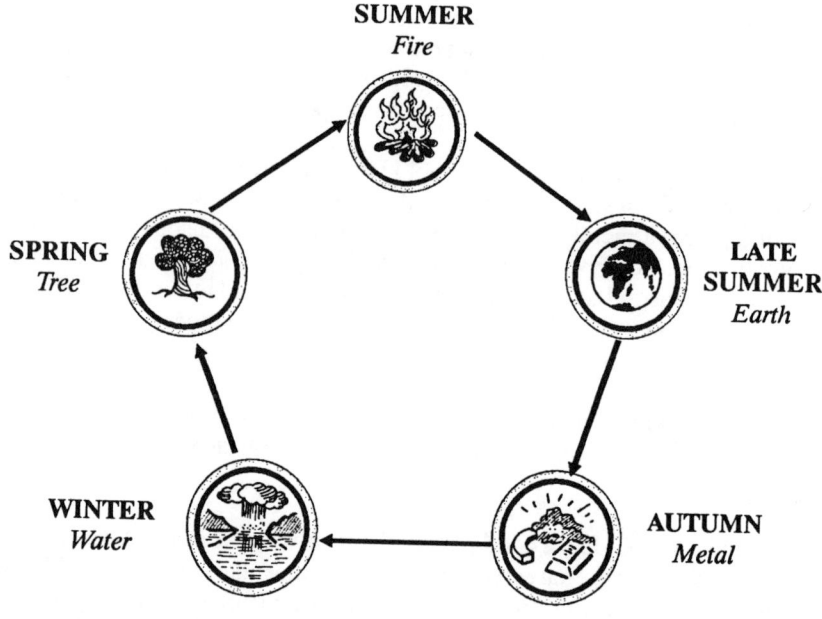

A circle is used to illustrate the five transformations to emphasize that everything is cyclical.

UNCULTIVATED GARDEN

In their wisdom, the ancients assigned an element to each stage to show the five types of ki. Spring is represented by a tree and called either tree or wood energy. A tree depicts growth and upward movement. Summer's element is fire, which shows activity. Late summer is a separate stage and has the element of earth, reflecting nature's abundant gifts. Autumn is represented by metal, hard and solid. And finally, winter has as its symbol water, which shows depth, spirituality and movement. Water is an interesting stage because it also allows for different kinds of water: still as in a lake, and frozen, or running as in a stream. Each of these kinds of water energy manifest in the winter months, as we will see later.

The pattern and its elements illustrate that energy continually moves from one stage to another, ever returning to these five transitions, and flowing forward in a spiral of evolution. This view is the essence of Oriental tradition: the basis of religion, medicine, and everyday life.

We can observe this consistent pattern of movement very easily when we apply it to the life cycle of a plant. Seeds sprout (tree stage); they grow and mature (fire stage); they flower and fruit (earth stage); and, finally, the life force concentrates itself back into a new seed (metal stage). After a period of dormancy and rest (water stage), the cycle begins anew.

The life cycle of human beings has the same spiral. Children are born and they grow (tree stage). They steadily move toward a time of great activity. These are the years of teen-age through young adult (fire stage). Here young people are usually fiercely involved in getting an education, finding a mate, securing a vocation, raising a family, obtaining a dream home, and so on. By the onset of middle-age this activity usually comes into harvest (earth stage). These years frequently offer a period of reaping the benefits of earlier efforts. By late middle age the kids have left home, life usually slows down, and people have time to read, travel, explore hobbies, and look within (metal stage). Finally old age is a chance for serenity and spiritual wisdom (water stage), before being born again and starting all over. Oriental perception of reincarnation is a natural aspect of the Five Transformations.

Within the human body there are cycles that closely parallel the stages of nature. This is where the Five Transformations gets very exciting and personal. According to ancient wisdom, our internal organs are more active, and can be more readily healed, during certain times of the year, day, and phases of the moon.

In a repetitious pattern of change we get many opportunities to grow and improve.

In the spring (March 15-June 15), early in the morning, and during the waxing of the moon (from new to full) the liver is most active. It releases its stored energy which, in turn, stimulates the forebrain and fills us with ideas and plans for the future. In spring we entertain such notions as to paint the house, plant a big garden, go on a summer vacation, or find a new relationship. Early in the morning we usually plan our day. And notice next time the moon becomes full, lots of new ideas may spring up. Tree stage gives us time to strengthen the liver.

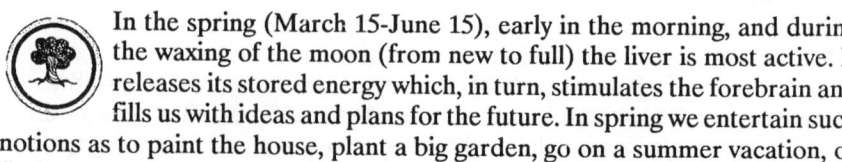
In summer (June 15-August 15), at mid-day, and for a few days around the full moon, the heart is very active. It stimulates blood circulation and energizes the organism even more than normally. In summer we are busy, busy, busy...painting the house, weeding the garden, zipping through a vacation, or falling deeper in love. Each day from about 10am - 2pm we experience the same fiery energy, that is IF the heart is functioning well. Maybe you have noticed that around the full moon you need less sleep and seem to be caught up in a flurry of activity. These fire stages are great times to get things accomplished, and to focus on strengthening the heart.

In late summer (August 15-October), during mid-afternoon, and after the full moon, the spleen and pancreas are most influential. (In Oriental medicine spleen/pancreas are considered as one organ.) The spleen stores blood for future needs. The pancreas secretes insulin which is necessary for sugar metabolism. Storing is the noteworthy function here. This is harvest time. House painting should be finished by now, the garden is profusely producing food (if you kept those weeds in control and remembered to water), vacation is over and school is starting, and you may be enjoying the benefits of the new relationship. Late afternoon is when we tie up projects and think about the bounty we want for supper. The period after the full moon is very often a time of reaping the rewards of ideas we planned a few weeks back. These earth stages are all good times to heal the spleen.

In autumn (October-December 15), during the evening or from the waning crescent to new moon, the lungs become more active. Autumn is the cold and flu season when the lungs are doing some fall house cleaning of old mucus. This is a good time to help them do it.

UNCULTIVATED GARDEN

Autumn supports turning within: metal stage. The garden is dying back, and that spring relationship is old hat: it is either strong or there is great pondering. We tend to overeat now and gain a few extra pounds of padding for winter. Evening energy encourages relaxing, and the all-American pastime...TV. And moon-wise, we are less active.

In winter (December 15-March 15), during the night and at new moon to shortly after, the kidneys can be readily healed. They are busy with cleansing of blood, a function which is enhanced by energy forced inward. The kidneys also regulate fluid balance in the body. Winter is a floating time between reflecting on the old year and planning for the new one; our attention is focused inward. It is a rather magical period when there is the least amount of yang physical light and the greatest intensity of yin spritual light.. Many religious holidays are during this water stage near the winter solstice, or shortest day of the year. In winter we are drawn to home, family, and hearth. It is a time to read, write and meditate. Late December, is a period when the winter may be cold and severe (frozen water). About the first week in January there is usually a great deal of moisture for the next three months (running water). In early January, we begin to formulate ideas from deep within (still water), that is, if the kidneys are not clogged. These ideas create the seeds which will be planted later in the spring. Late night is also rather magical. While most of us sleep, poets and artists work. And the new moon provides a chance for us to get caught up on sleep and look inward...before waxing energy charges us up again.

The Ancients, through the Five Transformations, have given us a tool for living healthy, balanced lives.

Various foods, colors, and tastes can also help each organ. By now you realize that these resources are available when they are needed. Nature produces the proper food for humans (and all creatures) at the proper time. The forces which form the foods, colors and tastes, AND the forces which influence the body, are the same.

The color green, the sour taste, and grains such as wheat, oats, and barley all have beneficial effects on the liver. These foods can be eaten in the springtime to enhance the functioning of the liver and to produce a light, upward feeling which is in harmony with the atmospheric energy of the season. Green-colored leaves, sour-tasting foods, and sprouting vegetables are all naturally abundant in spring.

Red-colored foods, bitter taste, and grains such as corn and red millet energize the heart. These summer-growing foods can be consumed to give the heart a boost. Much of the summer vegetation turns red and bitter tasting, leafy greens especially.

Yellow-colored foods, round foods, sweet taste, and grains such as millet, sweet rice, and sweet corn aid the functioning of the spleen and pancreas. These foods are abundant during late summer. In nature's bounty, the sweet taste manifests itself in berries, fruit, tubers/roots, and vegetables. Nuts, seeds, and grains also start to ripen by the end of this period.

White-colored foods, pungent taste, and grains such as rice enhance the lungs. Roots with high, above-ground vegetation, and leaves with serrated edges (such as the popular Japanese daikon) are also beneficial. These foods enable the lungs to cleanse, and are plentiful in autumn.

Black-colored foods, salty and mineral tastes, and grains such as buckwheat are all beneficial to the kidneys, as are beans, roots, above-ground vegetation which is low growing, sea vegetables, and fresh water plants such as watercress. These potent winter providers vitalize the body.

You can use this information daily, as well as seasonally. For example, if you eat a bowl of oatmeal and a generous helping of steamed greens for breakfast, the upward rising liver ki will be facilitated. Not so if you have greasy hash browns, toast and butter, and a thick slice of ham. The latter hits the liver like a lead weight and you will probably feel sluggish, at the very least. Just so, heart-supporting foods are valuable to include at lunch, and roots are advantageous in the evening.

Those sly Ancient Ones also discovered that within the body some organs have a complimentary relationship with each other. They work closely together, yet have somewhat opposite functions. Each pair includes a solid yang organ and a hollow yin organ. The liver is associated with the gall bladder, the heart with the small intestine, the spleen/pancreas with the stomach, the lungs with the large intestine, and the kidneys with the bladder. The Chinese further discovered that certain foods which are useful to one of the paired organs are also beneficial for the other. For example, sour-tasting foods help both liver and gall bladder. These relationships became a cornerstone of Oriental medicine.

When certain organs are malfunctioning, particular emotional patterns appear. For example, when someone eats too much animal food, fats, oils or hard crusty bread, this puts a burden on the liver. Quite often, excess fats can block the release of bile into the digestive tract, sending it into the bloodstream instead. Bile is a nerve irritant, so anger, shouting, irritability, and impatience are signs that the gall bladder and/or liver are not functioning properly.

Likewise, with the heart. Too much spicy food, sugar, tomatoes, or caffeine can give it excess energy. Excitability, excessive joy, laughter at inappropriate times, and a lack of calm serenity are signs of an overworked heart.

The spleen/pancreas is affected by refined sugar, fatty foods, eggs, chicken, and hard salty cheeses. Distrust, skepticism, the need for sympathy, and the habit of acting like a victim or martyr all indicate that a person has problems in these organs.

Refined flour products and dairy help cause excess mucus to collect in the lungs and to clog the large intestine. Depression results from a lack of oxygen going to the brain. Crying is the expression most used by people with this condition. Fear and loss of confidence develop when kidneys (and adrenals) are overstressed from excess salt, heavy fat deposits, and too much liquid.

Fascinating, isn't it? According to the Five Transformation Theory, personality traits develop over a lifetime, based significantly on dietary habits. With these observations, we can influence our emotions by changing our diet and life style. This is one of the focuses of macrobiotic practice.

APPLYING THEORY TO PRACTICE

In order to fully grasp the Five Transformation Theory we must experiment and observe. But please don't get neurotic about it. If we select food too intellectually rather than intuitively we can make ourselves very sick. The mind can rationalize anything. I know this because it has happened to me. My mind would have dialogues such as this: "Well its morning and spring, I better have tofu scrambled with amaranth greens." "No that's too yin for me now, it's a cold morning." "Gee, I really want a slice of bread." "Now, you know that's bad for your kidneys and makes you stubborn." Over-intellectualizing about food can drive you crazy. It is a common problem for students of Oriental medicine and macrobiotics. (Over intellectualizing I mean, not being crazy. Although everyone around you may THINK you are crazy.)

The Five Transformation perspective makes foraging a multi-faceted adventure. With the tool of this awareness, we can look at a plant and understand what organs it will influence. This is much easier than lugging five herb books to the meadow, only to be confused when an illness such as hepatitis has thirty-four possible herbs listed and you don't know any of them. Now you know that any edible wild green will do some good for the liver. A sour green will be especially good. You now have a basic foundation on which to build.

Just as our bodies are composed of many organs, so too are the plants made up of many kinds of ki. Don't expect to find ONLY sour greens in the spring. There is a predominance of them then because atmospheric changes which influence their growth also influence the liver. But in spring all the other elements of energy are working in plants, and in us. Same thing with each of the seasons. (Seasonal foods and their effects on the body are detailed in Part II, both in the introduction to each season, and in the sub-categories.)

To relate this concept to wild foods, it will be helpful to inspect a common plant. Let's use the dandelion as an example again. Go outside and look at the plant. The tops are leafy. "Hmmmm," you may say, "these will help the liver." You are correct. Now dig the root. You do and observe, "This resembles the intestines and will aid them and their complementary organ the lungs." Correct again. It is possible to eat the top greens and the root. When you do, it will help the liver, gall bladder, lungs, and intestines. "Hey, this is bitter," you say as you taste it. "Won't it activate the heart and small intestines as well?" Yes, it will. You are learning fast. You can now understand

UNCULTIVATED GARDEN

more fully why the dandelion is a systemic restorative, as mentioned in the Doctrine of Signatures.

If you want to get exacting about it, you can have the greens for breakfast and the root for dinner, or fix them both together for lunch. Generally speaking, you can enjoy dandelion any time of the day and all the organs will benefit.

One more observation. If you do this exercise in springtime, the roots are tiny and the plant's essence is primarily upward into the succulent leaves. Eaten in this season, the plant's ki naturally flows upward toward the liver. If it is late autumn, however, the root may be four times as big as it was in the spring, because in this season the plant is pulling nutrients, starch, and ki downward and in to stock up for winter. When you eat the plant, the ki naturally descends to the intestines (and affects its complement the lungs). What about summer? It is the same plant. However, the primal ki has by now cycled from the greens, to the flower, to the seed, and will be fairly well distributed between leaves and root. Due to the hot weather, its leaf structure has become condensed and the top growth is very bitter tasting, which implies a lot of power is metaphysically charging the earth. It can charge you too.

Because there is a connection between us and the plants (as well as everything else), we can forage and synchronize ourselves to optimal health. Like all critters, we evolved with a propensity to eat what was nearby and simple. This clever conservation of energy was a survival technique. It worked in the wild, before burger chains and candy counters were built atop the natural cuisine. We still forage for what's close, but the options are no longer attuned to our needs. Now we must use our intellectual understanding to get beyond complacent habits. This takes eagle vision.

The more we expand our mind, the more we are able to enhance our intuition. Paracelsus, the 16th Century physician and metaphysician, talked of the pursuit of knowledge as a two-fold path: intuition and experience. He believed the two must coincide. "The purpose of intuition is to reveal certain basic ideas which must then be tested and proven by experience," wrote Manly P. Hall in the book PARACELSUS, *His Mystical and Medical Philosophy*.[7] "Intuition without experience allows the mind to fall abyss of speculation without adequate censorship by physical needs... Further, experience is meaningless unless there is within man the power capable of evaluating happenings and occurrences."

According to Paracelsus, intuition is possible because of the existence in nature of a "mysterious substance or essence - a universal life force." He gave this many names, but was speaking of what the Orientals call ki and the Native Americans call "the spirit which moves within all things."

The Five Transformation Theory enables us to analyze with our left brain and to intuit with our right. It challenges us to become wholistic in our thinking. If you are interested in studying the Five Transformation Theory further, several resources are listed in the Reference Section.

INTUITION EXERCISES

VIBRATIONAL FIELDS

There is one more aspect of polarity which needs to be addressed. It is that all forms in the physical realm have a dense, or yang, physical body and a vibrationally active, or yin, etheric body. The two work interdependently to make life possible. Most people today only see the physical manifestation, but it is possible to develop your latent ability to sense the etheric half of the whole. The exercises below facilitate this development. The healthier a person becomes, the easier the task, although it requires spiritual opening of one's higher sensory centers, or chakras. If you clean up your diet, thoughts, and actions, do exercises to align your body, do some form of relaxation or meditative practice, and if you foster a reverence and appreciation for life, don't be surprised if you begin to experience many new and subtle vibrational or intuitive events.

People who can look back in time, such as Edgar Cayce and Rudolf Steiner, report that in the distant past, people lived in closer harmony with nature. There was less separation between humans, animals, and the plant kingdom. There was actually a time when people's thoughts affected how plants grew and blossomed. Humans saw soft, diffused images and there was less separation between the waking consciousness and the dream consciousness. We were more sensitive to cosmic influences then and the world of nature was a dynamic ocean in which people could see and experience the yin energies outside of yang forms. Rudolf Steiner explains these things in *Cosmic Memory*. (See the Reference Section for this and other works relating to the same topic.)

The Earth and its denizens were in their infancy then, but humans had to grow up. In order to become a mature life form, we had to distance ourselves from the spiritual world and develop our analytical abilities, just as a child grows to independence from its parents. Much medicinal and culinary plant knowledge dates back to that earlier time, when people really SAW. Later, it was a tale, or the tale of a tale, through which this information was passed on, although there remained a few seers - medicine people or shamans - who could still SEE, but who often had to undergo long training and great sacrifice to do so.

As adults, we can no longer return to a level of childhood openness and awareness. We see the world in a harsh physical form and attempt to look within it, separating and searching, seeking some generative principle behind natural science. It is now time that we, as a species, mature into the spiritual wisdom of old age and achieve a wholistic awareness. We must enhance our intuitive skills, as well as our scientific searchings, in order to truly understand our world and how to facilitate its healing and its evolution. This is our quest.

OBSERVING

The next time you forage take a notebook and pen. Sit down beside a particular plant or tree, and calm yourself by taking a few deep, long breaths. Then allow your self to become one with the surrounding landscape so you feel comfortable in your surroundings. Turn your attention to this vegetal being. Spend a full ten minutes meditatively focused on this plant. First observe the botanical structure. Are the leaves simple or complex? Are the leaf edges smooth, lobed, serrated, or other? What is the shape of the leaf: lance-shaped, heart-shaped, or other? Is the stem hairy or smooth? Is the branching alternate or opposite? (To answer these questions you may need to take a botanical guide along. *The Plantfinder* series is excellent and is listed in the Reference Section.)

UNCULTIVATED GARDEN 69

Now focus on various growth characteristics, as to their yin/yang nature. Utilize all your senses and observe plant structure, habitat features, texture, aroma, coloration, and taste (if it is an edible species). Next consider signatures and similars which speak to its usage. Also observe the plant in relation to its environment. What is its role there? Are there any insects on the plant? If so, which part are they on: flower, leaves, or stem? What are they doing? Are they pollinating, feasting, or other behaviors? Are there any indications of egg sacks, nests, insect damage, or other interesting clues? Take your time to thoroughly explore every aspect of this micro-environment. Keen observation is crucial for developing intuition. Make notes of what you see, and sketches if they will help you to observe more closely and remember what you discover.

When you are finished with these activities, take another five minutes and tune your awareness to more subtle vibrations. Observe what impressions or notions you have.

It is possible to communicate with plants. They don't chat with you the way a person would. They don't express themselves as does a dog, cat, or bird. The communication comes by way of sensations you feel or thoughts which pop up in your mind. It is easy to banish these away as "just my imagination," but what is imagination anyway? The study of theosophy and metaphysics further explains how communication is actually possible. The works of Rudolf Steiner, Michele Small Wright, and the Findhorn Society offer enlightening insights on this subject. Check the reference section for some of these books.

In the communication activity above I often have students work together as a group and then discuss their findings. The insights or messages are often quite similar. This is especially true with groups of children. Up to the time of puberty, children are quite sensitive to the subtle world which adults rarely perceive. If you have trouble with this last part, elicit the help of someone under nine years old.

GIVING THANKS

There are certain rituals and practices of earth wisdom which anthropology shows to have been universally practiced by medicine people and mystics of many ages and cultures. There seems to have existed a quiet yet solid body of wisdom about the plant kingdom and the elemental world, and an appreciation of the interconnectedness of all life. Our ancient forbearers realized that one must give before receiving. In a ritual which possibly dates back to the dawning of humanity, ancient medicine people would stand before a cluster of plants they wished to harvest for food or medicine. They would quiet their minds, and give thanks for the plant "brother or sister," and thank the spirit-that-moves-within-all-things, then give a precious gift such as tobacco, grain, or another substance which was sacred to them. All the while, these sensitive ones would listen to their still inner voice for guidance as to whether it was correct to harvest. Herbalists traditionally collected only what they needed, working lovingly to prune and thus assure strength and vitality for the remaining vegetal relatives. In this manner, a bond was formed between them and the plants. Ancient healers understood how a plant's qualities would manifest through the user.

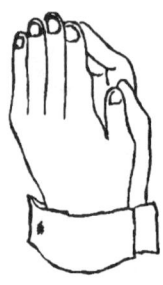

As modern-day foragers we can continue this sacred tradition of respect and thankfulness. When we do, a transformation often occurs in our linear thinking and there is a sense of becoming part of the intricate web of life. We can feel at one with the plant sister or brother in a unique and unexplainable manner. It is at this moment of connectedness that true communication is possible. This can manifest through a sense of knowing deep inside our being. We can "see-feel" the plant's yin vibrational field. As we practice, we can learn to perceive archetypal messages as well as an elemental communication such as, "This yarrow will stop external bleeding."

I encourage you to experiment and practice collecting in this traditional manner. Go outdoors to a good foraging location. Take as long as necessary to relax and to foster a sense of reverence and appreciation. Thank the community of a particular species from which you plan to collect. Then, gently harvest from each plant or tree of that species. Work as a gardener manicuring a royal garden.

When the treasure is brought home, utilize every particle of what was gathered, showing thankful appreciation as you clean, prepare, and finally partake of the gift.

BECOMING AWARE

As you develop the habit of collecting by first giving thanks and then asking permission, more subtle messages can surface. Often they come in the form of insights. For example, one day I was hiking in the woods and a young juniper cedar seemed to beckon me near. I quietly thanked it, savored its beauty, then gave a prayer of blessing. I proceeded to randomly pick a few boughs and put them in my herbal medicine pouch for later use. As I trimmed, a clear image about the responsibility of receiving entered my mind. I was given the thought that when a person receives any gift, he or she needs to be appreciative and thankful. I was certainly thankful for this cedar. To show it, I collected from the branches so as to enhance the tree's symmetry. The gift of this insight was profound at the time, for I had recently been disappointed by a gift I'd received when I'd expected something different instead. It is this type of timely message which I often receive while foraging in a thankful manner.

Working my way around to the far side of the tree, I spied a plastic survey ribbon tied snugly around a bough cluster. It was as though someone had taken a person's hand and tightly secured a band around all five fingers. I could feel the discomfort. I imagined how my hand would feel in such a position. The pain would totally distract me. This tree was suffering, and that's why it had caught my attention. I pondered the situation. The tag was to mark a survey line. A surveyor had been insensitive when he tied the ribbon. I untied it, moved it up about one inch and loosely re-tied the ribbon around a single branch (analogous to moving it up to one's wrist, like a bracelet). I sensed a rush of relief and love. Both of us gave and both received. I'll long remember that interaction.

While outdoors, tune your consciousness to the world around you. As city dwellers, we learn to shut out hundreds of annoying sounds, ignoring even a loud police or ambulance siren. Then we go to the woods and thrash about noisily, our minds roaming somewhere far away. Before walking into a natural setting, or even into your backyard, take a few deep breaths. Allow the tension to flow from your body and let the carnival in your head subside. Look around and appreciate. Then, pay attention to what's in your view. You'll perceive birds, animals, insects and maybe even begin to perceive the plant people. Be an antenna and see what happens.

ATTENTIVENESS TO HOUSE PLANTS

One New Year's Day, I got a particularly strong desire to spend the following year learning from the "plant people." I was thinking about wild foods and herbs. A few hours later, I was doing the dishes when some plants hanging in the window seemed to shout at me. "Look at us," they seemed to call. "We're a mess and thirsty. If you want to learn from the plant people, you must begin with us. We need our dead leaves removed; we need to be watered, dusted and misted; we need nutrients; and some of us need to be re-potted." I stopped what I was doing and attended to EACH plant. I rearranged where many sat or hung. They looked lovely in their new locations and I felt more in harmony with them. Maybe the message came from the plants or from my subconscious mind when I happened to glance at the them and finally notice their plight. The effect was that various phenomena coalesced at a point in time enabling me to experience insight and growth.

The next day, the book *The Secret Life of Plants* by Tompkins and Bird appeared unexpectedly in my life. First, I found a copy on the floor in the hallway where it had fallen from its spot on the bookshelf. Next, I saw it on my favorite reading chair (left there by a visitor). Two days later, a friend and I were having lunch. Out of the blue, she said that she was reading the book and thought I would enjoy it. That was enough coincidence. I was having a busy week but realized it was time for me to read that book. The opening chapters contained amazing scientific findings about communication with house plants, and supported some of what I had experienced a few days earlier with my house plants seeming to call to me.

UNCULTIVATED GARDEN

When I watered the plants on that New Year's day I decided to give them a shower because they look so dry and dusty. When I did so, I experienced a sudden rush of excitement and the sense that all the other plants wanted a shower too. This event gave me the idea for an experiment. Find a house plant which needs watering, one which does well when sprayed or misted. Put it in the shower. Run cool water over it, and pay attention. Can you feel a charge of energy as the water runs over the plant? Imagine how the roots and stems respond as they begin to absorb the water. Don't intellectualize the process; simply feel. Try the same awareness exercise the next time you add plant food or dust your plants.

It is necessary that all our house plants be well cared for. I once went to the home of a well-meaning lady who preached a great deal about loving your neighbor. A dying spider plant hung in her front window. It was withered, most of its leaves dead, and the soil was hard as a rock. This woman talked of love, yet her plant was dying from lack of it. Many of us simply forget, as she and I had, that our house plants are dependent upon our nurturing. Love starts in the home with simple things. By attending to these things in our most noble manner, we change the world.

FEELING KI

Every living entity has its own unique vibrational field, just as each person has a unique fingerprint. Each plant species has a specific frequency, and within that species, individual plants emit subtle energy differences which are influenced by habitat, growing conditions, and other factors. Sensitive people can feel, and sometimes see, these frequencies. By paying attention to the vibrational fields, ancients could detect whether a species was poisonous or benevolent.

In this exercise you will work on tactile sensations. I suggest you practice with poison ivy. Poisonous plants often radiate strong vibrations. Poison ivy certainly does, as if to say, "Leave me alone." Carefully stand a few feet from a patch of

it. Quiet your mind and rub your hands briskly together until the palms become warm, then blow on them and feel the effect of your breath. Is it warm? Cool? Feel the tingle of the breath touching your palm. Repeat the brisk rubbing, a bit longer this time. Blow again. You should be able to feel a stronger sensation. Now your hands are more sensitized. When you're ready, slowly pass them two or three feet over the tops of the ivy leaves. Be careful not to touch the plant. If you are extremely sensitive to poison ivy, try a different plant. Yarrow and mint are good ones because they too have active yin fields. Do the pass-over several times and observe the feeling on your hands. Next, try a different species nearby, then a tree, then a rock, then a person. What do you feel? What do you notice? Focus on variations in heat, osmotic pressure, and other subtle sensations on your hands. Attempt to ascertain a frequency. If you practice this exercise regularly, your receptivity may dramatically increase in just a few weeks.

MUSCLE TEST

Applied Kinesiology, also called muscle testing, provides a fascinating way to test various foods and obtain immediate feedback as to their beneficial or harmful effects. This is a relatively new technique based on discoveries (done primarily behind the Iron Curtain) which reveal the body as composed of an intricate system of bio-electric charges. Different organs have either a positive or a negative field, and these fields, taken together, determine the frequency of the total vibrational field surrounding a person. Plants also demonstrate the same kind of bio-electric fields, with different parts of a plant producing differently charged fields. Roots, for example, show a different field than a leaf, flower, or stem. The entire vibrational field of a person or plant is the sum of the many smaller fields of its parts integrated into one larger field. When these larger vibrational fields of two life forms come into contact with each other, the smaller component fields change. If you encounter a plant and feel a vibrational force, you do so because your field and the plant's are interacting and changing.

UNCULTIVATED GARDEN 75

Because of this, there is a change in your overall field even before you consume something! This is why a person can benefit from simply wearing an amulet or pouch containing a medicinal herb around his or her neck.

To do muscle testing, find a partner and stand face to face. Have him extend his left arm straight out to the side, allowing the other arm to hang comfortably. Place your left hand on your partner's right shoulder and your right hand close to his left wrist.

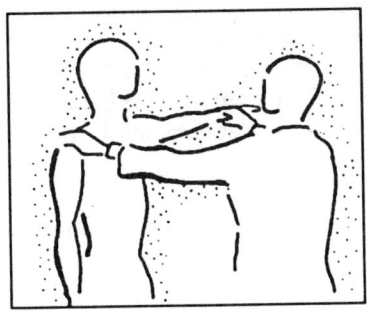

Ask your partner to resist as you quickly move your right hand downward. Only an inch or so is necessary. If the muscle is weak, the arm will go down quickly. If it is strong, the arm will lock. This is not an arm-wrestling match. Be gentle. This first check is the base line by which to assess changes in muscle strength.

To really get a feel for how quickly the muscle can weaken, begin the test by giving your partner a cup of white sugar to hold in his resting right hand. Have him bring this to a point just below his naval, at the hara or intestinal center. Test the left arm again, asking your partner to resist your downward pressure. You will be amazed at what happens. White sugar is harmful to the body, and in that amount, will immediately weaken your partner's arm strength. This will give you both a feel for what is happening. Next, have your partner hold an edible part of a wild plant in his resting right hand and bring it close to his hara. If the arm muscle becomes weak when the plant's vibrational field is near your partner's abdomen, the plant is weakening for him. Try the test with various amounts of the plant to determine whether a larger volume has a more weakening or strengthening effect. Try various other wild edibles, even toxic plants if you wish. (Be sure to allow your partner a chance to rest his out-stretched arm when it starts to get tired.) It is interesting to try more subtle things such as checking a food cooked, then raw, to see if there is a difference. Try herbal remedies and chemical medications. This can be great fun once you get the hang of it.

I found that after a few weeks of muscle testing, I was able to hold a plant and sense, before testing, whether it would be strengthening or weakening to my system. The muscle test is merely a feedback method to fine-tune awareness.

Applied Kinesiology can be an extremely exacting technique to check for medicinal benefits, as well as desired foods. I have given a very brief overview. Many variations have been developed to make these tests more precise, and the techniques can be studied. If you want to use this method as a serious diagnostic tool, you can read up on these refinements in the books suggested in the Reference Section.

CAUTION: Use this test along with a positive identification of the plant.

TASTE TEST

A Mohawk medicine man with whom I apprenticed taught me an old practice which far preceded identification books. I will share it. It is very simple and will help you learn from your own experience.

For this experiment, forage on a relatively empty stomach. Find a cluster of a species which you already know is edible and give thanks. Take a tiny piece of the plant and place it in your mouth for a minute or two. Turn your attention inward. Is the taste pleasant or harsh? Do you notice any effects, such as it making your lip or tongue tingle? Does it seem safe to eat based on knowledge and intuition of your systemic condition? If yes, then proceed to chew and swallow the little sample. Wait at least one hour before eating anything else and observe yourself closely. What do you feel? If you feel any nausea, cramping, dizziness, et cetera, then avoid eating any more. This will likely occur only if the edible shows several signs of extreme tendency.

It's a great test. Simple as it is, the exercise offers a profound method for developing a deep connection with many edible and/or medicinal species. Medicine people used it with a foundation of knowledge. To be safe, do this taste test only after checking color, odor, texture, habitat, and so forth for extreme yin or yang, and after keying the plant out with an identification book. Tasting a toxic plant, even in this manner, can be foolhardy. Remember that common sense, coupled with observation, are the primary tools for survival and evolution of knowledge.

Sometimes we think we have positively identified an edible, but in fact it is something different. I see this repeatedly at workshops where students and I scrutinize the flora, and then I send everyone out to collect what we just studied. Several people will come back with bags of strange plants which don't even resemble what I asked them to harvest. We discuss this as a group and use it as a learning opportunity. Even the common dandelion, as familiar a weed as it is, can fool a forager. For several years I would start to harvest this weed and then pause because I was not sure it was dandelion. Sometimes the leaves are small, reddish, and deeply serrated. At other times the leaves are large, lightish green, and hardly serrated at all. Growing conditions strongly affect dandelion's features. Even with this ubiquitous weed that everyone knows, it is possible to make mistakes. The taste test helps with mistaken identity, and allows forewarning about something which is too extreme for your condition.

SUMMARY

Each of the above exercises involves slowing down, and keenly focusing on observation. In the fast pace of urban life very little importance is placed on such matters. For example, someone who sits for hours and watches a bird build its nest might be called lazy, but the ancients taught that the path of careful observation is the key to greater understanding.

PART II - PRACTICE

*Man can live a true life
only with nature*
                Masanobu Fukuoka

SEASONAL PLANTS AND THEIR USES

An Introduction

Okay, here we go. Part I provided theory. Part II is practice. This section is to help you learn how to simply and successfully use the edible vegetation which you find and identify. Remember, this book is a how-to manual, not an identification guide. Many excellent guides are list in the Reference Section. Please acquire a good one, or several, and use them. This book takes you the next step.

In this section we explore each season of the year, what is happening energetically in the environment, and how we can cook for maximum harmony.

MAKING USE

I have noticed with myself, and others, that it is very easy to get carried away when we collect. We have so much fun harvesting that we come home with baskets full of food. Somehow this volume magically doubles in size when it gets to the kitchen. I have often marveled at this phenomenon. But the plants frequently lay on a corner of the counter until they spoil. This often happens because SIMPLE ways to utilize them are not known. I have attempted to address this issue and provide many easy culinary suggestions (as well as

some which require time and determination). These ideas and recipes are offered as aids to stimulate your creativity and to encourage experimentation. By using them, you will hopefully waste very little uncultivated produce, and have a good time trying new treats.

SIMPLE FOOD: A BLESSING

Uncultivated produce can best manifest its healing and cleansing powers when it is prepared in a simple, wholesome manner which employs many natural ingredients.

Since 1975, I have continuously refined my diet and experimented with cooking wild ingredients in many ways. This all started in August of that year when I spent two weeks canoeing in Canada. During that meditative retreat, I had a strong vision to stop eating meat. I loved meat, and up until that point beef was the mainstay of my diet. But I easily stopped eating it because of the vividness of the message. Gradually over a seven year span, I also weaned myself away from sugar, eggs, milk, cheese, salt, and processed foods. Now I enjoy a way of eating which is much broader than before, although that may seem hard to believe. I eat primarily whole grains, vegetables, beans, grain sweeteners, fruit, and a daily supplement of wild foods from land and sea. Because of eating a wholesome grain-based diet I moved beyond illness. Now I utilize 80-90% organic food, a varying proportion of which includes numerous wild ingredients. I follow a macrobiotic, wholistic approach of eating in harmony with the changing seasons and geographic locale. This parallels how humans have eaten for hundreds of thousands of years. The commitment takes some effort. However, I feel very energetic and mentally clear, I need less sleep and accomplish probably twice as much as when I consumed a more typical modern diet.

The recipes I selected for this guide reflect my style of vegetarian cuisine. The use of meat, eggs, dairy products, sugar, and artificial substances has been avoided. What's left? Look and see.

UNCULTIVATED GARDEN

140 SPECIES

One hundred and forty different wild foods are listed in this section, according to their season of edibility. These species were chosen because most of them grow well in temperate climates, and because they are relatively easy to find and identify. The 140 are my favorites. Most are delectable resources which can be readily blended into one's daily diet.

Throughout this section I have listed recipes according to the plant part (greens, flowers, fruit and berries, nuts and seeds, grains, roots and tubers, mushrooms). Before each set of recipes are tidbits of information about each. Not all of the plant parts are featured in each seasonal chapter. For example, I have not included flowers in the Winter chapter because they are not blooming then. When they do appear, the most prominent part for that season will be dealt with first, followed by the others in order of decreasing occurrence for that season.

MODERATION, PLEASE

When you try any uncultivated food for the first time it is imperative to eat a small to moderate amount. If you remember only one message from this book, please remember this one. Many wild foods are powerful, medicinal sources of vitality. Most people are not accustomed to such potent food. When eaten, wild foods can cause our junk-food-saturated bodies to cleanse themselves of artificial substances and toxins. This discharge may be beneficial, but it is wise to cleanse the system slowly. If you overeat a new food, an allergic-type reaction may occur such as stomach-ache, rash, dizziness, rapid heartbeat, or other symptoms. Usually you will feel stronger and pleasantly content after eating wild produce, but not always. So go slowly in order to insure positive results.

REMEMBER

Several comments bear repeating in case the reader is focusing only on this section.

THINK FIRST: Use common sense when foraging. The still voice within is the most important teacher of all. You may make some mistakes, but common sense ought to keep you from making major ones, especially if you employ resource guides as continual companions.

KNOW THE CAUTIONS: Please refer to the PRECAUTIONS AND TIPS at the end of the Getting Started chapter. There can be dangers in wild food foraging as well as joys.

GIVE TO RECEIVE: There is are many far-reaching benefits when we harvest with loving concern. We must be careful gardeners as we forage. A sudden rush of greedy weed-collecting could deplete our local resource of strong, healing foods. As we collect, let us make our presence in the natural setting a gift. It is important to forage in a manner which insures that a bigger crop will be there next year, and for generations to come.

OBSERVE: Pay attention to whether any subtle messages, insights or new thoughts come from the plants when foraging or after eating. The plant kingdom wants us to clean up our actions and begin to live in balance with the natural order of the universe.

BACKYARD FORAGING: Collecting wild treasures can be a fairly simple endeavor, especially if you have a little land. I suggest you gradually transplant various herbs, berries, fruit and nut trees, and "weeds" into your yard or garden borders. Seeds from wild root crops such as burdock and wild parsnip can be collected in late summer and scattered in appropriate places. Many herbaceous species can be dug from the wild and replanted in your home environs. Thus, you create an edible landscape design.

The neighbors may think this is crazy. But make it attractive, maintain a strong conviction, and educate others as to the benefits. With numerous resources nearby, it is quicker to harvest in the backyard than to travel to the supermarket. Making use of what is at hand is an intelligent approach to foraging.

FEEDBACK

Please send me your favorite recipes and interesting experiences. I am always eager to learn new ideas and may include some, along with your name and town, in a second booklet. By sharing our insights we can further our knowledge and expand our perception. There is always much to learn from the plant kingdom. Write to:

DEBORAH LEE
c/o HAVELIN COMMUNICATIONS
P O Box 5630
Takoma Park, MD 20912

SPRING FORAGING

Tree Element

The magic of springtime touches all of Earth's creatures. Let's look at what happens in the environment and at the parallels which occur inside our bodies. This information will help us understand the role of spring foods.

At the onset of spring, rapid expansion occurs because of negative ions which have concentrated near the Earth's surface during winter. These begin to rise upwards to meet positive ions which have been hovering in the atmosphere. When they meet, a chain reaction is set in motion, causing electrical storms to develop as these two sets of ions collide. The process charges the soil as well as moistens it. Seeds that have been dormant all winter now start to sprout. Their new, upward growth is facilitated by the polarity of the ionic effect, as well as by warmer temperatures and increased sunlight. Upward energy manifests everywhere through a surge of growth and activity.

All living beings feel the change and become quite active. I certainly do. From middle to late March, it is virtually impossible for me to remain inside. I'm like a caged animal needing to break free. I prefer to be in the sun exercising, foraging, and most of all preparing the garden for a summer's abundance of vegetables. Our lawn and garden provides baskets of produce before I even plant a seed. Dandelion greens and roots, thistle, garlic mustard, nettle, wild onions, plantain, wild lettuce, dock, and day lily shoots are all likely to be "weeded" then brought inside for lunch or dinner.

Spring is the season of greens: succulent, young greens which are rich in iron, vitamins A and C, and other nutrients. Their abundance surrounds us, even in urban places. Dozens of species of so-called weeds are edible during the ten to twelve weeks of spring. (In cool, mild climates and mountain regions this season is longer.) Every week or so, some species bolt to flower and get too tough or bitter-tasting to enjoy in salads or as a pot herb, but five or six other species are likely to pop up in replacement. This is a very exciting time to forage.

In order to understand the systemic effect of greens, roots, and other spring foods, we must look inside ourselves. The body goes through a tremendous change from winter to spring. During winter, the orthosympathetic nervous system (ONS) triggers the body to pull warmth inward and downward to the internal organs in an effort to stay warm. This collecting and condensing function is facilitated by eating root vegetables all winter because vertical roots are formed by spirals of the same downward, collecting energy. In the new weeks of spring we still need to stay warm. Edible roots are great to dig soon after the soil has thawed. Plants such as burdock, thistle, and dandelion get an early top growth which allows them to be spotted in sparse landscapes. They can be easily dug. As spring advances we want to reduce our consumption of internally warming foods and begin to have greens. Nature provides the information we need by example. New sprouts and greens start to take over. These new leaves and stalks contain a lot of expansive (yin) upward and outward energy. The yin growth occurs at the same time the body begins its internal spring changes. As temperatures warm up outside, the parasympathetic nervous system (PNS) switches gears and stimulates energy to be pulled from internal organs to the periphery, like an internal air conditioner. Our bodies go through these amazing adaptations and most of us never notice.[8] If we munch the leafy greens which are naturally prolific in spring, we help the PNS do its job. We can easily stay in harmony with environmental patterns if we partake of uncultivated food.

Later in spring, flowers, fruit, and mushrooms grow. These further help to draw heat outward because they are a manifestation of even more expansive (yin) ki, as explained in Understanding Balance.

The ONS naturally switches dominance to the PNS in spring. If we eat heavy, yang foods such as red meat, eggs, cheese, winter grains, and a lot of root vegetables, our diet is at cross purposes with the naturally occurring transition. Eating leafy greens in early spring can help us feel light, cool, and buoyant.

Our style of spring cooking can also assist the PNS, and we tend to naturally do this. We crave fresh salads and light cooking. Raw or pressed salads, light

UNCULTIVATED GARDEN

boiling, steaming and quick water saute are some other styles of preparation which help cool the body.

Until fairly recently in history, people naturally ate what was growing around them without thinking about the effect. Sometimes when we study the role of food and healing it gets quite confusing. There is no need to intellectualize or worry about what to eat in order to acclimatize to nature's whims; simply look around and observe what is available and in what proportion. Then follow your instincts. Study nature, not nature books, to reveal the way to stay comfortable in any climate.

Springtime's uncultivated foods have other functions as well. They provide abundant nutrients, leafy greens in particular. Wildlife and humans traditionally need a boost of vitamins and minerals after a long winter of precious little vegetation. Many varieties of edible greens act as a liver and blood purifier. In modern times these little gifts are especially helpful because the liver collects toxins from chemical additives, environmental pollutants, and medication, as well as animal foods and oil. Spring greens are a godsend. A serving a day keeps the doctor away.

When we comprehend the dietary and medicinal purpose of spring weeds, we can more fully appreciate that spring is a great time to head for the open fields, meadows, streamsides, and the backyard.

In this section, tips and spring-style recipes are designed to help you utilize commonly found produce. Many recipes are provided for leafy greens because they are the most abundant.

GREENS

Many spring greens taste sour. Sour flavor, coupled with rapid expansive growth and high levels of iron, enhance the new leaves with a unique ability to cleanse the liver and the bloodstream. Further tonic benefits come from the high content of vitamins A, C, and D. Some greens are also rather bitter. This taste shows that the plant has blood tonic and circulatory system benefits as well as liver cleansing functions.

The order of arrival of spring greens varies according to climate and habitat. Growing conditions drastically affect flavor and the appearance of a plant. In many temperate regions, hardy greens stay fresh all winter, then have a spurt of growth when the weather gets warm and sunny. These species usually grow fast, seed early, and get tough quickly. They include mustard family, wild lettuces, wild onion and chives, and thistle.

Harvest periods for each type of leafy green also fluctuate with the climate. Dandelion greens, for example, are delicious in Kansas from late February to early April. After that they become very bitter. In the mountains of Pennsylvania, these greens unfold about the end of March and are often tender and enjoyable all summer due to cool weather. After a summer rainy spell, the dandelion leaves may grow large for a few weeks and taste quite mild.

A common problem for the new forager in spring is collecting leaves and shoots when they are a bit too old, tough, and bitter. I remember one spring in Kansas when my friend, wild food author Kelly Kindscher, and I, decided to host a wild edible pot-luck dinner in the park. This was the last time I ever did this without teaching a class first. People brought old greens, boiled and topped with butter. They were awful, bitter and tough. This mistake can stifle one's enthusiasm. Stick to tender edibles. Take a nibble when you collect to decide if they are delectable. When greens ARE harsh, however, they do not always need to be passed by. "The stronger the flavor, the better the medicine," says Native American medicine man and wild food connoisseur, Rolling Thunder. At this stage greens can be lightly boiled, the water discarded, and the greens boiled again in fresh water. This is called "boiling in several waters" and is commonly recommended in foraging guides and cookbooks. A secret I've found to reduce harsh flavor is to simmer bitter greens with 1/4 to 1/2 teaspoon miso and a cup of water.

The following list offers common spring greens, plus important cautions. Many of these species grow throughout regions of North America and Europe. All are easily to identify.

UNCULTIVATED GARDEN

COMMON SPRING GREENS
Early Spring

Bracken Fern *	Cleavers	Nettles
Broad-leaf dock	Comfrey	Ostrich fern
Catbrier	Curly dock	Plantain
Cattail	Dandelion	Watercress
Chicory	Japanese knotweed *	Wild onion family *
Chickweed	Miner's lettuce	Wild lettuces
Chives	Mustard family	Wintercress

☞ * Ferns - Eat at young fiddlehead stage. Not all fiddleheads are delectable. Check a reference guide before collecting.

* Japanese knotweed - Use young spikes only, and cook. Rapid growth, purple coloration, and sour taste all indicate extreme yin and toxicity; eat in moderation.

* Onion family - Be certain the familiar onion/garlic smell is present. Death camas somewhat resembles wild onion or garlic, but does not have the odor.

COMMON SPRING GREENS
Mid to Late Spring

Amaranth	Mallows	Sheep sorrel
Cattail	Mint family *	Shepherd's purse
Coltsfoot	Milkweed *	Thistle family
Glasswort	Peppergrass	Violet leaves
Grape leaves	Pokeweed *	Watercress
Lamb's quarter	Purslane	Wood sorrel

☞ * Milkweed - If milkweed is placed in the refrigerator or placed under cold water, the bitter flavor is locked in. Rinse in warm water. Be certain that you have milkweed, not dogbane. The latter resembles milkweed when both are about 3-12 inches tall. Milkweed has soft, light-colored and slightly furry leaf undersides. Dogbane is more shiny and has red on its stem.

* Mint family - The family includes scores of square-stemmed, aromatic plants such as spearmint, lemon balm, catnip, peppermint, and many more.

* Pokeweed - Collect it up to two feet high only, and cook. After that stage, a purple tint and rapid growth show extreme yin and toxicity.

SPRING ROMANCE SALAD

To highlight a spring meal, concoct a fairy-tale salad by combining various young, tender leaves and/or flowers. This tossed salad is great for camping trips.

Catbrier - tips
Cattail - lower stem
Dandelion - flowers
Day lily leaf - spikes
Grape - leaves
Lamb's quarter - leaves
Mint family - leaves
Plantain - leaves

Redbud tree - flowers
Red clover - flowers
Sheep sorrel - leaves
Watercress - sprigs
Wild lettuce - leaves
Wild onion - tops/bulbs
Wood sorrel - leaves
Violet - flowers/leaves

Use some of the following and add lettuce, if desired.
Rinse, toss, and top with a favorite dressing.

REDBUD SORREL SALAD

The sour flavor of both these ingredients stimulate the liver and help to dispel stagnation. (Caution: wood sorrel is high in oxalic acid and is best eaten in moderation.) There is no need for dressing on this seasonal dish; its flavor makes it taste as though dressing had already been added.

1 c. redbud tree flowers
1 c. wood sorrel leaves

Rinse, toss together and serve as a side dish.

UNCULTIVATED GARDEN

SPRING PRESSED SALAD

A pressed salad is made by using a light pickling process which involves salt, pressure, and time, all of which have a yangizing or concentrating effect. The process alkalinizes the raw foods and renders them more digestible. Place desired vegetables in an earthen crock, deep bowl, or pickle press, apply a heavy weight such as a gallon jar full of water and allow to press 2-8 hours. Stir at least once. Combinations of ingredients are limited only by one's imagination. Two of my favorites are:

#1
1-2 c. watercress sprigs, cleaned
3 c. cabbage, sliced thin
1 c. red cabbage, sliced thin
1/4 c. toasted sunflower seeds

#2
1/2 c. violet leaves, sliced
1/4 c. grape leaves, sliced thin
1 c. watercress sprigs, bite-size pieces
2 or 3 cattail stems, peeled, bite-size pieces
2 c. garden lettuce
1/2 c. red cabbage, finely shredded

Toss ingredients for 2-3 minutes with 1 teaspoon sea salt, or 1/3 cup umeboshi vinegar, until moist. Press, then serve with favorite dressing or eat plain. (Add seeds at serving time.)

NETTLE POTAGE

Thanks to Anna Bond for this delicious country recipe. Anna's potage is a colorful dish as well as tasty. She is careful to not overcook her greens and cause them to lose their color.

1 1/2 c. black soybeans
1 c. young nettle tips, chopped
3" strip kombu

1 c. leeks, finely sliced
miso or tamari to taste

Soak the beans and kombu in 6 cups of water overnight. Pressure cook for 1 hour. Remove the kombu, cut it into 1" strips, and return it to the pot. Add leeks and nettles and simmer about 5 minutes or until tender. Season with miso or tamari.

SPRING SAUTE

Use a small amount of oil. Remember the liver needs to cleanse during spring. Eating too much oily food stifles this process and can make us feel irritable. The following recipe can be changed to include literally hundreds of variations of greens and vegetables. It is also a simple campfire dish.

2 c. nettle tops
1 c. tender curly dock leaves, cut on diagonal
1/2 c. onion or chives, diced

1/8 t. dark sesame oil (or other oil)
1/8 t. tamari or soy sauce
1 T. toasted sesame seeds (optional)

Wash greens. Slice dock greens and separate nettle leaves from their stem or cut into bite-size pieces. Set aside. Brush the bottom of heavy skillet or wok with oil. When hot, stir in onion or chives and saute 2-3 minutes. Add the wet greens. Saute 2-3 minutes, stirring. Add a few drops of tamari to taste. Cover, reduce flame, and simmer until tender yet still bright green in color. Serve topped with sesame seeds.

Toasted sesame seeds: Rinse the seeds briefly and drain. Place into a heavy skillet which is already hot (no need for oil). Heat over a medium flame, until moisture evaporates. As they start to get dry, stir constantly to avoid scorching. Reduce flame to prevent high flying seeds from popping all over the kitchen. Roast until seeds easily crumble between the thumb and forefinger and a rich, nutty aroma is apparent. Remove from heat, cool and store in an air-tight glass jar. Sprinkle on sauteed dishes, salads, cooked grain, et cetera.

VARIATION:
- Experiment with other young spring greens such as: broad-leaf dock, violet, dandelion, lamb's quarter, milkweed, mallow, pokeweed, chicory, amaranth, wild lettuce, mustard greens, day lily leaves, chickweed, comfrey, and watercress (add cress near end of cooking).

NETTLE-TOFU CASSEROLE

Tofu (soy bean curd) is an appropriate spring food. Its yin qualities help draw stagnation out from deep inside.

4 c. nettle
1 lb. tofu, diced
1 onion, cut in half moons

1-2 t. tahini
tamari or soy sauce
wild bergamot (or oregano), to taste

Steam the nettle 5 minutes (to get about 3 cup), then chop. Heat oil in a heavy skillet or wok. Saute onions 2-3 minutes; add tofu and saute 4-5 minutes longer. Add nettle and saute 2 minutes. Place in a baking dish and stir in seasoning. Bake 15 minutes at 350°. Add tamari to taste, and bake 5 minutes more. Top with black sesame seeds that have been toasted.

VARIATIONS:
- In place of nettle, use dock, lamb's quarter, young milkweed tops, violet leaves, amaranth, mallow, wild onion, or add fresh watercress just before baking.
- Instead of tamari and tahini, use 2 tablespoon white miso for a dynamic cheesy taste.
- Fill your favorite pie crust with the uncooked ingredients to create tofu quiche.
- Saute mushrooms (wild or domestic) with onions and proceed with the recipe.

STUFFED GRAPE LEAVES
With Mock Tomato Sauce

In the following Greek dolmades recipe, a mock tomato sauce is included as a substitute for traditional tomato topping. Many people have an arthritic reaction to nightshade family plants (tomatoes, bell peppers and potatoes), so this tasty variation is given. Tomatoes can be used, if desired. I make a Greek dinner each spring when grape leaves are full-sized and light green. The traditional meal includes Spring Romance Salad.

1 med. zucchini, chopped fine
1 T. olive oil
1/2 c. wild onion, minced (or 2 med. onions)
1 t. dill

2 T. lemon juice
4 c. cooked rice
20-30 grape leaves (young ones from late spring/early summer)
Tomato sauce, with basil (or Mock

Heat oil in a heavy skillet. Add onion, then zucchini and spices. Saute 2-3 minutes. Add lemon juice. Stir, season with sea salt and add about 1/2 cup hot water. Simmer 1 hour, or until water is nearly evaporated. (If necessary, add water during cooking time.) Remove from heat, mix in rice and adjust seasoning to taste. Place a spoonful of the mixture on a grape leaf. Roll, beginning at the stem end, folding in the sides. Line a baking dish with the stuffed leaves. Add topping. Bake at 350° for 30-40 minutes.

MOCK TOMATO SAUCE:

1 med. butternut squash
1 large red beet
1 large carrot
3 med. onions

4 T. sauerkraut juice
2 T. sesame oil
2 t. bergamot *

Chop squash, beet, carrot, and onions into large pieces. Place in a cooking pot. Add 2 cup water and boil until well cooked. Blend ingredients, stir in spices and sauerkraut juice to taste. Simmer 10-15 minutes. Spread on top of the grape leaf rolls and bake.

* Bergamot flowers and leaves need to be collected in summer.

SPRING TAMARI PICKLES

A small amount of salt pickle can be eaten at the end of each meal to create a slightly alkaline condition in the stomach and aid digestion. Many cultures eat salt pickles. The following is a Japanese-style preparation.

When collecting spring cattails, reach into the water at the base of the plant and cut above the root. These can be collected for several months until the cattail is ready to flower. While you are in the marsh, peel off the outer leaves to reveal a soft, tender core. Only this part needs to be taken to the kitchen. (Outer leaves can be dried and used for weaving projects.) Combine the pickle ingredients and let them sit for 24 hours. Serve 1 or 2 at a time.

>   *1 c. cattail stalks, 2" pieces*
>   *1 c. water*
>   *1 c. tamari or aged soy sauce*

VARIATIONS:
- Try violet leaves or young day lily leaves.

KNOTWEED-APPLE PIE

Japanese knotweed is a unique plant which somewhat resembles rhubarb in flavor. It is yummy in desserts, as explained here. When cooked, the color is light green and tastes better than it looks. Hide it with a top crust. Collect the Japanese knotweed sprouts in early spring when the plant is about 1-4 feet tall. The plant grows extremely fast and shows many yin characteristics. This recipe utilizes a long cooking time to help create balance.

1 part Japanese knotweed, 1" pieces *1/2 c. water*
3 parts golden delicious apples, *cinnamon, to taste*
quartered *vanilla extract, to taste*
1/4-1/2 t. sesame oil *your favorite pie crust*

Saute the apples and knotweed in sesame oil. Add water and seasoning. Simmer for about an hour. Pour into a partially-baked pie shell and top with another crust. Bake at 350° for 45 minutes or until the crust is golden brown.

VARIATION:
- Make a compote dessert by simmering the ingredients and omitting the crust. Serve warm. Top with toasted sesame seeds.

ROOTS AND TUBERS

Eating roots helps thicken our blood and generate warmth. For that reason they are best eaten in winter or very early spring before the tops appear. As the tops sprout, use roots and tops, if both are considered edible. The plant's maximum nutrition and potency is going into the new leafy growth. By eating the root and the top, the plant's full strength is obtained. On a more subtle level, use of entire plants allows us to view life from a wholistic perspective.

COMMON SPRING ROOTS AND TUBERS

Burdock
Cattail
Chicory
Dandelion
Day lily
Great bulrush

Jerusalem artichoke
Prairie turnip
Toothwort
Wild ginger (for seasoning)
Wild parsnip

Look to the Autumn and Wintering Foraging sections for other root and tuber recipes. Recipes provided below are particularly suited to spring. During the erratic weather common to spring's awakening, I like to add fresh roots to soups, sauteed vegetable dishes, casseroles, fried rice or pressure-cooked grain.

UNCULTIVATED GARDEN

COUNTRY WHEAT AND RYE

The following recipe is a favorite in our home any time of the year. Wheat and rye are traditional European grains and are also a pleasing staple.

1 c. whole spring wheat berries, soaked 6-8 hours
1/4 c. rye berries, soaked 6-8 hours
1 1/2 to 2 c. water
pinch of sea salt
1/2 c. wild onions, diced (tops and roots)
1/4 c. celery or young day lily leaves
1/2 c. wild roots and/or tubers, diced *
dark sesame oil or other oil
tamari, soy sauce, or salt

Place wheat and rye berries in a pressure cooker with water and sea salt. Pressure cook for 50 minutes. (For boiling instructions, see VARIATIONS.) Remove and allow to cool. Heat a small amount of dark sesame oil in a skillet. Saute onion root for 1-2 minutes. Add onion tops, day lily, and carrot. Saute 1 minute. Add cooked wheat and rye berries, sprinkle a little tamari on top, and cover. Reduce the flame to low. Cook until vegetables are tender. Season with a little more tamari, if desired, and mix. Saute 1-2 minutes more. Remove and place in a serving bowl.

* Roots and tubers: day lily, Jerusalem artichoke, Wild carrotwild carrot, parsnip, burdock, prairie turnip, thistle, or toothwort.

VARIATIONS:
- To boil: use 2 1/2 to 3 cup water and boil on low for 1 hour or until done.
- Instead of young day lily leaves, use the tender inside stalk of cattails. Their ambrosia-like flavor adds a special delight.
- Other replacements for day lily include milkweed tops, thistle stalks (shaved free of spikes), violet leaves, or other mild greens such as nettle.

YANG PANCAKES

The combination of buckwheat and wild vegetables makes this recipe very yang and invigorating.

Filling:
1/4 c. wild or domestic onion, sliced
1 c. greens, cut in strips *
1/4 c. wild roots or tubers (or domestic carrots), diced *
pinch sea salt

Batter:
1 c. buckwheat flour
1 c. w.w. pastry flour
1/2 c. water (adjust amount if necessary)
pinch sea salt
sesame (or other) oil - for frying

Heat a heavy skillet and coat with 1 teaspoon oil. Mix all ingredients. Ladle onto grill as for pancakes. Cook until done on both sides. or, slightly saute filling, then add batter and cook. Garnish with edible wildflowers, such as violet.

* Greens: plantain, violet leaves, nettle, milkweed (steam first), lamb's quarter, cleavers, chickweed, wild lettuce, et cetera.
* Roots and Tubers: Jerusalem artichoke, day lily, Wild carrotwild carrot, wild parsnip.

RAMP MISO

If you live in wild leek (ramp) country, you are lucky indeed. I was visiting Luc Bodin and Anna Bond in Vermont. They have a hillside of ramps and enjoy them year-round. I was delighted when they shared their ramp miso with me. Luc told me how they drove to Massachusetts one spring to get 45 pounds of South River miso. To it they added wild leeks and let the combination sit 6 months. They have been enjoying the garlic-like flavor for several years. Here's how they said to make it.

Choose freshly-picked spring ramps with large well-formed bulbs. Wash them well and steam them to fix their color and enzymes, but not to the point of the bulbs becoming translucent. Cool them immediately by plunging them in ice cold water. Slice and layer them with aged miso in a crock or glass jar. To 1 quart miso, add approximately 1/2 cup ramps. Wait until Thanksgiving and use to season soups, stews, and other recipes.

FLOWERS AND FRUIT

Some flowers and fruits appear in spring, although summer is prime time for both. You may recall from the diagram of plant energetics in the Understanding Balance chapter, that flowers are an extreme yin manifestation of plant growth, while fruit is the most yin. Fruit produces seed, which is the most yang structure of a plant. In this process, yin changes quickly to yang and a new cycle unfolds. A more in-depth discussion of the effects of flowers and fruit is given in the Summer Foraging section. Strong yin in flowers and fruit acts to cool the body by thinning the blood, as well as by facilitating the PNS to draw out excess heat. As we observe that only a few edible flowers and berries are available for harvest in early spring, we again can learn from nature what foods will best enable us to adapt to this season and to the local climate. Eating a moderate amount of both flowers and fruit helps us to slowly adjust to seasonal warming trends.

FLOWERS: My favorite use of edible flowers is to sprinkle them as a garnish on salad, in beverages, or in cold soup. But I also make flower arrangements that nourish my soul with their beauty. There is something about the perfect beauty of a flower that can cause even the most grumpy among us to smile. I feel it is important to include flowers in one's life for they speak to us of hope and love. I've been deeply impressed by the work of Dr. Edward Bach, who in the 1930's brought flower essences to the attention of Western culture. These essences heal our spirits, which seem to long for attunement with the life force of nature. Flower essence remedies have been known to herbalists for centuries. They offer interesting study.[9] In my opinion, flowers (eaten in small amounts) can work miracles at various levels of our being.

Pick flowers in the morning when they are still fresh with dew. In the morning, earth force energy rises up to the leaves and flowers. Avoid the temptation to nibble any flower. First determine whether it is edible.

COMMON SPRING FLOWERS

Black locust
Clover family
Dandelion
Elderberry *
Miner's lettuce

Mustard family
Redbud tree
Rose family
Violet
Wood sorrel

* Elderberry - flowers and berries only; leaves and twigs are poisonous.

ELDER BLOSSOM FRITTERS

Large elder umbels are easily gathered in meadow habitats or beside streams. Children like this snack and might be easily encouraged to gather the blossoms and mix the batter.

6-8 elderberry blossoms
1/4 c. w.w. flour
1/4 c. rice flour
1/4 t. cinnamon (optional)

1/2-2/3 c. beer (or fruit juice)
1/4 t. sea salt
1 T. kudzu (heaping)
2 c. safflower or sesame oil

Mix all the dry ingredients in a bowl. Slowly stir the beer in. Dissolve kudzu in small amount of cool water and blend it into the mixture. If the mixture is too thin it will be unmanageable, so adjust the liquid accordingly. Dip flower umbels into the batter and deep fry in hot oil. Serve as a dessert with jam, maple syrup, peanut butter, or other favorite topping.

VARIATIONS:
- Use red clover or roses.
- Commonly, elderberry blossom fritters have been made with orange juice in place of beer, then dipped in powdered sugar.

UNCULTIVATED GARDEN 103

ADDITIONAL SUGGESTIONS

- Use flowers as garnishes to make even a dull meal delightfully memorable.
- Add flowers to salad recipes just prior to serving.

FRUIT: In spring the fruit which grows in temperate climates is small, compact, and yang, traits which are a response the cool weather. In summer, temperate climate fruits are larger, juicier, and more yin. These plant adaptations to the weather help us maintain heat equilibrium and gently acclimatize our systems to summer conditions.

One of the first fruits to appear is the wild strawberry. This wild relative of the commercial strawberry is about the size of a small pea. It is red and grows on a tiny plant low to the ground. These are all signs of yang tendency. Even though it is the most yin part of the strawberry plant, the berry is a substantial food and is far more yang than its large, watery, hybrid cousin. Even a small amount of wild strawberries, or other wild spring fruit, can give us a lot of energy - which is good because collecting takes a while! My experience is that spring wild fruits and berries contain a potent life force which makes eating them as filling as four to five times the amount of commercial strawberries.

Personally, I think the best way to eat spring fruit is to nibble it fresh from the plant. The recipes below offer additional ideas.

COMMON SPRING FRUITS AND BERRIES

Gooseberry   *Mulberry*
Juneberry *   *Strawberry*

 * Juneberry - commonly called service-berry in many regions.

BERRY COMPOTE

Mulberries have a subtle flavor which is perked up by tart gooseberries. Both ripen about the same time and are also pleasant tasting in pies. Wild strawberries are tiny and take some dedication to pick.

1/2 c. apple juice
1 c. mulberries
1/2 c. gooseberries
1 c. domestic strawberries (or 1/4 c. wild)
1 T. arrowroot powder, kudzu, or cornstarch
1/4 c. walnuts, roasted and finely chopped
pinch sea salt

Soak mulberries for 10 minutes in water with 1/4 teaspoon sea salt to dislodge any insects. In a cooking pot add juice, gooseberries, and sea salt. Simmer 2-3 minutes. In a separate bowl, dilute arrowroot or kudzu with a little cool water. Add to the juice, stir, and add mulberries. Simmer until thick, stirring constantly. Remove from heat and add walnuts. Serve warm or cool.

VARIATION:
- Simply mix fresh fruit and roasted walnuts for a fruit cup.

JUNEBERRY PARFAIT

In this recipe I use commercially sold agar-agar seaweed instead of gelatin. It has the same quality and solidifies without refrigeration. In addition the seaweed contains more vitamins and minerals, and it helps remove toxins from the body. Agar-agar can be purchased at a health food or Oriental store. Substitute gelatin, if preferred.

1 qt. fruit juice (apple or other)
pinch sea salt
5 T. agar-agar flakes (or 2 bars)
1 pt. juneberries
1 t. tahini (or peanut butter)

Rinse and sort juneberries. Place juice, sea salt, and flakes in a pot. Mix well. Bring to a boil, reduce flame to low and simmer 5-10 minutes, or until the flakes are dissolved. Remove one cup of liquid and allow it to cool in a separate bowl. Add juneberries and simmer the remaining mixture 1-2 minutes and pour into

UNCULTIVATED GARDEN

four individual parfait-type glasses. Set in a cool place until both mixtures are almost firm. In a blender or mixing bowl, blend tahini and the reserved cup of firm juice until it is smooth and creamy. Top each glass with this and add a garnish of mint leaf, orange twist, or a spring flower.

VARIATIONS:
- Use any spring, summer, or autumn fruit you might use for Jello.
- Half water and half juice can be used for a less sweet taste. If more sweetener is preferred, use barley malt, rice syrup, maple syrup, or other.

See Summer and Autumn Foraging sections for further uses of fruit.

MUSHROOMS

I mention mushrooms only briefly because I am leery of teaching people about mushrooms and fungi. This family of extremely expansive foods combines many yin factors of growth and therefore can be tremendously poisonous. There is an inexpensive, compact book entitled *How To Recognize 30 Edible Mushrooms,* by Antoine Devignes, published by Barron's of Woodbury, New York. I suggest it for both beginner and seasoned mushroom hunters.

In the infinite balance of nature, if a plant is extreme enough to be toxic, an equalizer usually grows very near by. So a yin species of poisonous mushroom would have within eyesight an equally yang balancing agent, quite possibly a root. By learning these secrets, we may become more adept foragers. The mushroom patch offers a good place to start.

Springtime is likely the best season to eat the quick-growing, expansive, uplifting mushroom. I advise they be cooked to yangize them.

Morel mushrooms are my favorite. They are easy to identify, but elusive. I've spent countless days in April or May looking for the tasty morsels. If I'm lucky enough to find a big colony, I leave some for deer and other critters, plus enough to insure that next year's hunt will be better. Then I string some up with needle and thread and hang them in the attic to shrivel and dry. They can also be dried overnight in an electric dehydrator. Every collecting book says something different about morel conditions and habitat. A person needs a bit of luck and communication with nature, to do well. Then, be secretive regarding where they were found, lest fellow foragers may clear the patch.

WATERCRESS MUSHROOMS

Morels are exceptionally well-suited for this recipe. If you come home empty-handed, commercial mushrooms are good, too. These hors d'oeuvres can be served hot or cool. They get better as they sit a day, so make enough for tomorrow's lunch.

16 large mushrooms
1-2 c. watercress, chopped fine
1 T. sesame oil
1 T. shoyu

1 clove wild onion, minced
1 T. mirin or cooking sherry (optional)
1 T. spicy mustard

Preheat oven to 450° F. Clean the mushrooms and remove the stems, or, in the case of morels, cut them in half down their length. In a small bowl, mix watercress with all ingredients except the oil. Fill the mushrooms with this mixture. Brush the baking dish with sesame oil and bake the stuffed mushrooms for 15 minutes.

BARLEY-BEAN SOUP WITH MUSHROOMS

Barley has a prevalence of spring energy. When eaten, it helps rid the liver of animal fats, dairy foods, and excess in general. This recipe is delicious cooked in a Dutch oven over the campfire.

1/2 c. barley, pearled
1/4 c. kidney beans
1 bunch wild onion, diced
4 stalks cattail, peeled & diced

1/2 c. wild mushrooms, sliced
5-6 c. water
1/4-1/2 t. sea salt
1 t. miso, to taste

Wash beans and soak 5-10 hours. Discard the soaking water to cut gaseous effect. Wash barley. In a cooking pot, layer the onions, barley, and kidney beans. Cover with water. Bring to a boil, reduce the flame, and simmer about one hour or until the beans are almost cooked. Saute mushrooms in a little oil and add them along with the cattail stalks and salt. Cook 10 minutes more.

VARIATIONS:
- Use celery instead of cattail.
- In late summer, puffballs are delicious in this recipe.

ADDITIONAL SUGGESTIONS

- Morels are scrumptious when rolled in cracker crumbs and egg and fried in oil. This idea is an old rite-of-spring family recipe from my parents and grandparents, as well as many other mid-west families.
- Saute mushrooms with oil or butter, either by themselves or with spring vegetables such as peas and scallions. Cover with wine or cooking sherry, simmer 1-2 minutes and thicken with kudzu, arrowroot, or cornstarch. Serve as a side dish or over noodles.
- Use in omelets, scrambled eggs, or quiche.

SUMMER FORAGING

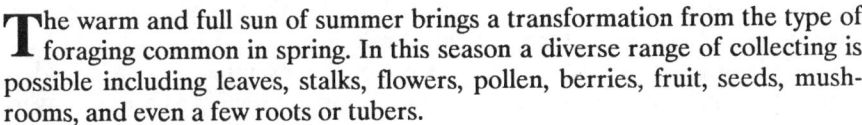

Fire Element

The warm and full sun of summer brings a transformation from the type of foraging common in spring. In this season a diverse range of collecting is possible including leaves, stalks, flowers, pollen, berries, fruit, seeds, mushrooms, and even a few roots or tubers.

The majority of plants have matured to the point that leaves and stems are no longer succulent and enjoyable. A few plants still provide leafy greens all through summer and autumn (such as violet and comfrey). However, the edibility of these depends significantly on climate. In cool, moist regions several varieties of greens can be collected all summer (such as dandelion, lamb's quarter, and amaranth) for use in salads. In hot, dry climates the same leaves get very tough, dry, and bitter.

Bitter flavor is common in summer. It speaks of elements which nourish the heart and circulatory system. As a result, this is a good time to strengthen this system.

Berries, fruit, spices, aromatic herbs, mushrooms, and flowers take to summer heat. These, as you may remember from the discussion of plant parts in the Understanding Balance chapter, all contain varying degrees of expansive or yin energy. When eaten, these foods stimulate the parasympathetic nervous system which draws heat from the central organs and carries it outward to cool the body. Activation of this internal cooling system helps us adjust to hot weather. Certain yin foods such as fruit and berries also work to thin the blood and further cool the organism.[8]

Cooling foods grow in proportion to environmental conditions. For example, northern prairie regions have 6-8 weeks of hot weather sandwiched between a long, severe winter. During this period yin characteristics manifest in the plants so that aromatic herbs, flowers, and fruits are at a peak. The humans and animals which forage there can adjust to this abrupt climatic change fairly easily. When temperatures quickly cool, vegetation changes to foodstuffs which create greater warmth. Even if we don't eat wild foods, but just observe the seasonal changes and adjust our eating habits accordingly, we benefit from the natural spiral of change and adaptation.

Summer's produce is abundant and diverse, making the season a great time to forage. For this reason, beginning foragers sometimes dream of living entirely off the land. Of course, this is possible; civilizations have done so for hundreds of thousands of years. Realistically though, the task is time-consuming, requires knowledge and skill, and a supplement of wild meat and fish. For most of us, foraging is practical on a small scale. I prefer, for example, to enjoy garden produce throughout most of the summer and look to foraging as a good way to thin the weeds which grow amongst the vegetables. I also stock up for winter by collecting and drying leafy greens, berries, and fruit. And I gather herbs, spices, and medicinal plants for year-round use. In this manner, foraging is a playful part of my regular routine. My need to test survival skills is met by taking backpacking trips and relying primarily on what can be found. I will take some grain, noodles, and nuts, plus a few supplemental items (salt and cooking oil), and forage for the rest. CAUTION: This can be risky if one is unfamiliar with the habitat and only starting to study edible plants. But it's a great way to focus on learning!

HERBS AND SPICES

In most temperate climate locales, herbs and spices grow prolifically during summer and they can easily be collected. You may like to do as I do and take short forays once a week in July and August. Numerous riches can be collected in an hour and brought home to be used fresh or dried. I love herb treks. The anticipation of year-round use makes my adventure all the more purposeful. When I use the stash later on a cold, desolate day I remember the joy of the outing and a spiral of pleasure continues.

If you wish to dry herbs and spices, select mature plants at their fullest prime. Harvest them in the morning just after the dew has evaporated from their surfaces. (Plants collected when they are wet with dew have more tendency to mildew.) Early in the day, the atmospheric energy is rising upwards (see Five Transformations) so the fullest essence of ki is in the flowers and greens. Any old herbalist will tell you morning is the time to pick aromatic plants. Hang them upside down in a warm, dry place such as an attic or garage. In some cases it works best to spread plants across a non-metal screening material like nylon or muslin which has been stretched tight on a frame. (Avoid the temptation to use old aluminum screens because the wire can adversely affect a plant's taste.) When I lived in Pennsylvania, our residence was cool and moist all summer. Herbs and spices would mildew before they ever dried. During that period I started using an electric food dehydrator and was very pleased with the results. Flowers and leaves would dry overnight. They retained their color and content to an impressive degree.

In order to preserve leaves and flowers properly, they need to be dried at temperatures below approximately 115° F. When herbs are completely dry, place them in an air-tight container, label them as to content and date, and store them in a cool dark place such as a pantry. Try to store leaves whole rather than crushed to retain maximum aroma and flavor. Properly stored, summer-collected plants can offer years of enjoyment, although potency diminishes each year.

Herbs and spices can be a very important resource year-round for seasoning, beverage, and medicine when they are utilized wisely and with a degree of moderation. In winter, we need to eat foods which will keep us warm. Herbs don't. However, it is easy to eat too much constricting, heat-producing food even on a vegetarian or macrobiotic diet. Our condition can quickly get too yang or tight. Instead of reaching for extreme yin such as beer or extra dessert, the delicate use of herbs naturally curbs those desires and helps bring balance as well as diversity. Commonly, we get tired of hibernating and growl like a bear at family or friends. These are the times when a breath of summer flavor and aroma can help us relax. The delicate use of herbs and spices enhance a meal so it seems almost like a summer picnic.

COMMON HERBS AND SPICES FOR BEVERAGE AND/OR TRADITIONAL MEDICINAL USE

Alfalfa - leaves
Bergamot - flowers and leaves
Blackberry - leaves
Camomile - flowers
Catnip - leaves
Coltsfoot - leaves
Comfrey - leaves
Clover - flowers
Dewberry - leaves

Elderberry - flowers
Horsetail - tops
Juniper - berries
Kinnikinik - Labrador tealeaves
Labrador tea - leaves
Mint family - leaves
Mugwort - leaves
Mullein - leaves
Nettle - leaves and stems

Persimmon - leaves
Pine family - needles
Pineappleweed - flowers
Plantain - leaves
Raspberry - leaves
Rose - flowers and leaves
Strawberry - leaves
Sweet goldenrod - flowers and leaves

☞ - Volatile plant oils will be damaged if the leaves and flowers of aromatic plants are overheated. Boiling an herb will often destroy its delicate flavor and beneficial effects. To use for tea, boil water first, then pour it over the dried leaves or flower tops. Steep for 10 to 20 minutes. Use glass, ceramic, or enamel preferably. Metal pots distort the taste.

Macrobiotic dietary advice recommends to be moderate in the use of expansive spices and herbs, especially in cool climates. I agree. I also look at the many types of spices and herbs which naturally dot the countryside and caution that we not allow our intellect to downplay the important role these plants play. They bring the gifts of flair and diversity to our meals.

There are many uses for summer-collected herbs beyond food, beverage, and medicine. Dried herbs and flowers can be gathered and made into attractive flower arrangements which last all winter and share their beauty in numerous ways. Aromatic herbs and flowers bring sensory pleasure when dried and combined for potpourri. Small potpourri bundles make unique and very personal gifts, as do small jars of hand-picked herbs. It is important to look at various aspects of foraging. There are many types of food. Food for the eyes and nose can be just as strengthening as food (or medicine) for the stomach.

UNCULTIVATED GARDEN

EVERYDAY BEVERAGE

This tea, as its name implies, is suitable for daily use. I use it regularly in the winter because nettle acts as a blood purifier and strengthener. Kukicha, or bancha twig tea, is a caffeine-free substitute for leaf tea and is quite enjoyable. Less caffeine naturally occurs in the stems of the plant variety utilized, and no dye or chemicals are added in the processing. Purchase kukicha in natural food stores.

> *1 pt. spring or well water*
> *1 t. (heaping) dried nettle leaves, crushed (if fresh use 1/2 c.)*
> *1 t. (heaping) bancha twig tea*

Add bancha to water. Bring to simmer and cook for 10 minutes. Avoid boiling. Add nettle. Turn off heat and steep 15 minutes. If desired, gently reheat to a hot but drinkable temperature.

VARIATION:
- Instead of bancha twig, use New Jersey tea or a commercial black tea.

HERBAL RELAXANT

Some summer herbs have mild sedative effects and are helpful if one is feeling tense from stress (or other contracting, yang conditions). Camomile and various mints, including catnip, are helpful, so keep them handy. They are not to be used everyday. Drink them only when necessary. The tea is a nice nighttime relaxant, unless insomnia is due to excitability from expansive yin such as spices, sugar, coffee, et cetera.

> *1 pt. spring or well water*
> *1-2 T. dried herbs (camomile, mint, or catnip)*

Use earthenware, glass, or an enamel pot. Bring water to a boil. Remove from the heat and pour it over the herbs which have been crushed (to release extra potency). Steep for 10-15 minutes. Serve warm.

GENERAL MEDICINAL TEAS

The following are easy to find and provide commonly needed remedies. Prepare as above. Use 1 oz. of dried, crushed herbs to 2 cups water.

- Blessed thistle - general tonic; also soothes stomach, heart, mammary glands, uterus, and blood.
- Comfrey - general soothing effect on entire body; helps pancreas regulate blood sugar; aids in cell proliferation, thus helping to heal wounds.
- Dandelion leaves - liver and blood tonic, general systemic restorative.
- Kinnikinik - for kidney and bladder infections.
- Plantain - antiseptic, astringent, general systemic booster. Drink the tea or pour it (strained) onto antiseptic bandage and apply to wound.
- Sage - astringent, antispasmodic, antihydrotic. It calms the mind and helps meditation. Also it helps eliminate mucous congestion in respiratory passages and stomach.
- Yarrow - anti-bacterial, astringent, stimulant, good for early stages of flu or colds. This can be prepared as a tea and used on wounds as mentioned for plantain.

COMMON HERBS AND SPICES FOR COOKING OR CONDIMENT

Basil - leaves
Bergamot - flowers and leaves
Caraway - seeds
Coltsfoot - leaves
Day lily - flowers
Ground juniper - berries
Elderberry - flowers
Lamb's quarter - seeds
Mint family - leaves
Mustard family - flowers and seeds

Rose - flowers
Peppergrass - seeds
Sage - leaves
Sassafras - leaves and root
Spicebush - twigs and leaves
Shepherd's-purse - seeds
Staghorn sumac - seeds
Thyme - leaves and stems
Wild onion family - leaves and seeds

BAKED TROUT

Seasonally abundant, fresh-water fish can be very delicious when seasoned with various herbs which likely grow along the shore. Experiment with herbs when cooking bass, trout, perch, sunfish, or other fish harvested from lake or stream. Fish are rich in protein and can be enjoyed in a number of ways. The following is a very simple preparation.

1 trout, 1 to 2 lbs.
1 T. sesame oil (or other)
Choice of herbs (mint, basil, bergamot, juniper)
1 t. tamari (or salt to taste)

Clean the fish, slitting the underside of the belly from the head down to the tail. Grease a baking dish and place the fish in it. Brush the fish top with remaining oil, sprinkle tamari or salt lightly over it, and sprinkle about 1/4 teaspoon of one or more herbs inside. Try bergamot and basil together, or mint and dillweed alone, or together, or crushed juniper berries. Pre-heat your oven to 350°F and bake until tender. Bones can be lifted free more easily after baking. Garnish and serve.

VARIATIONS:
- Stuff with rice, diced onions and herbs. Place on a bed of the same stuffing and bake.
- For camp cooking, wrap in aluminum foil or moist clay, and bake over campfire coals.

TABOULI

Tabouli is a Middle Eastern favorite and can be made many ways. I've included the traditional use of tomato. Tomatoes are members of the yin, nightshade family and some people are sensitive to its toxic properties. For this reason, a non-tomato variation is also given. Prepare the recipe three or four hours before serving so flavors mingle.

1 1/4 c. boiling water
1/4-1/2 t. sea salt
1 c. uncooked bulgur
1/4-1/2 c. fresh mint leaves, minced *
1/4 c. lemon juice
3 T. olive oil

1 c. fresh parsley, minced
1/4 c. violet leaves (optional)
1 med. carrot shredded
2 med. tomatoes, diced
lettuce leaves

Stir salt into boiling water. Add bulgur and mint. Stir thoroughly and cover for 30 minutes. As this rests, combine lemon, olive oil, parsley, violets, and carrots. Let this mixture sit for 20 minutes, then stir it into the bulgur. Add tomatoes and toss. Chill for 2-4 hours. Serve on a bed of lettuce with mint sprig or edible flowers as a garnish.

* Many wild mint varieties have a very strong flavor. If you are unfamiliar with the taste, use only a small amount. More can be added at the end, if desired.

VARIATIONS:
- Instead of tomato, use 2 cucumbers, diced.
- Instead of violets, use another edible green.
- Add a clove of garlic, minced, for additional flavor.

SPICY OATMEAL CEREAL

Spicebush is a substitute for cinnamon, and similar in taste. In temperate climates it allows us to focus better in the morning than if the more dispersive cinnamon or nutmeg were used. This recipe is nice for children's cereal.

1 c. rolled oats
3 c. water
pinch sea salt

1/2 c. fresh blueberries or other fruit
2-6" spicebush twigs

Break twigs into several pieces. Place the water, salt, and twigs in a pan and simmer for 15 minutes, remove the twigs, add the rolled oats and cook over low heat, with a flame deflector under the pan to avoid scorching. When the oatmeal is cooked, stir in the fresh fruit. Remove from heat. Dish into bowls and serve.

VARIATIONS:
- If using dried raisins or other dried berries or fruit, add these to the water at the beginning of cooking.
- Top with seeds or nuts. Toasting renders them less oily, more easily digestible, and more flavorful.

ADDITIONAL SUGGESTIONS

- Mustard, shepherd's-purse, or peppergrass seeds are tasty seasoning for soup and stew.
- Bergamot flowers, dried and crushed through a thin sieve, taste similar to oregano. They are well suited to Italian recipes. (See the recipe for Mock Tomato Sauce in Spring Section.)
- Day lily flowers are a Chinese delicacy and will thicken a stir-fry vegetable combination, sauce, or soup.
- Juniper berries can be placed in a tiny cheesecloth bag and simmered for seafood, fish soup, or meat stew, or mixed with cabbage and pounded into sauerkraut.
- Caraway or peppergrass seeds enhance the flavor of bread or rolls.
- Dried rose petals are pleasant in salad, steeped for tea, or added to black or twig tea.

FRUITS AND BERRIES

More than any other foods, these thin the blood and cool the body when temperatures soar (although eating too much fruit can cause one to feel hot and sticky). As spring moves into summer, fruit and berry varieties change from being small and compact (such as strawberries) to large, plump or juicy, and more yin (plums, apples, or peaches). The latter are particularly abundant during the hot days of late summer.

Whether the bounty is foraged from natural areas, the orchard out back, or the market down the road, it makes sense to preserve and store some fruit for winter. After spending numerous summers stifled in a hot kitchen canning and freezing gallons of fruit, I learned to appreciate the pre-canning tradition of drying fruit to preserve it. I've used a solar food dryer and a commercial electric food dehydrator, but prefer a drying house heated by a wood fire for optimal success. Fruit needs to be dried at 110-140° F and should be kept at a somewhat constant temperature. Sun drying is possible in hot, dry climates. To do so, spread the berries (whole) or fruit (cut very thin) on nylon mesh or muslin that has been stretched taut. Cover with cheesecloth to keep bugs away and place in a hot location which has good ventilation and is safely away from disturbance. Bring the fruit inside at night. When dry, store in air-tight glass jars or ceramic crocks.

COMMON SUMMER FRUITS AND BERRIES

Apple - late summer
Blackberry - mid summer
Blueberry - mid to late summer
Black cherry - late summer
Chokecherry - late summer
Crab apple - late summer
Currant - late summer
Dewberry - mid summer
Gooseberry - early summer
Elderberry * - late summer

Grape - late summer
Huckleberry - mid summer
Juneberry - early summer
May apple - mid summer
Mulberry - early summer
Raspberry - early summer
Sandhill plum - late summer
Strawberry - early summer
Wild cherry - mid summer
Wild plum - mid summer

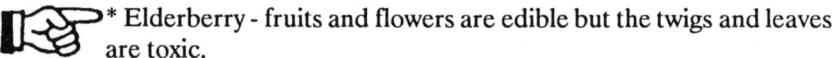* Elderberry - fruits and flowers are edible but the twigs and leaves are toxic.

* The following three recipes are great basic preparations which I use repeatedly.

UNCULTIVATED GARDEN

BLUEBERRY PIE

Makes one large or two small pies. Use your favorite crust.

FILLING:
4 c. blueberries, washed
pinch sea salt

1/4 c. water or juice
1/4 c. arrowroot powder
1/4 c. syrup, rice or maple

In a saucepan, add blueberries, sea salt, and water. Bring to a boil, reduce heat, and simmer 2-3 minutes. Add sweetener. In a separate bowl, dilute arrowroot powder with a little cool water. Stir into the hot berries, and keep stirring to prevent lumps. Cook until thickened. Allow this mixture to cool as the pie shells are made. Poke several holes in the bottom of the shells with a fork. Bake 10 minutes at 350°F. Add filling to shells. Bake at 350° for 30 minutes, or until crust is golden brown. Allow to cool, then cut.

BASIC CRUST: (for 2 pies)
4 c. w.w. pastry flour
1/4 t. sea salt

1/8-1/4 c. corn oil
3/4-1 c. cold water

Combine the flour and salt. Slowly add the oil, sifting with your hands to mix thoroughly with the flour. Gradually add water and form the dough into a ball. Knead 2-3 minutes. Allow the dough ball to sit for a few minutes, then divide it in half and roll it out on a floured board.

VARIATIONS:
- In place of blueberries, use one of the following: juneberries, mulberries, a mulberry/gooseberry combination (2:1 ratio), apple/elderberry combination (3:1 ratio), cherries (with more sweetener and 1 teaspoon lemon juice), black cherries, or other favorites.

CHERRY-WALNUT CRUNCH

Use commercial or homemade granola. Use seasonal fruit.

2 c. cherries, washed and pitted
pinch of sea salt
1/2 c. apple juice (or other juice)
2 T. arrowroot powder or kudzu root

1 1/2 c. granola
1 1/2 c. roasted walnuts, chopped
2 T. barley malt or maple syrup

Combine cherries, sea salt, and juice. Mix arrowroot powder with a small amount of cool water and add to the fruit mixture. Stir constantly and cook for several minutes on a low flame until thickened. Remove from the heat and spread into a baking dish. Combine granola, walnuts, and sweetener. Spread evenly on top of the fruit. Bake uncovered at 350° until the topping is golden brown.

VARIATIONS:
- Instead of cherries use: blackberries, raspberries, blueberries, mulberries, a mulberry/gooseberry combination (2:1 ratio), apples, apple/elderberry combination (3:1 ratio), juneberries, plums, or sandhill plums.
- Try other nuts or seeds.

CORNMEAL-WILD FRUIT MUFFINS

Most summer fruits and berries work well in this recipe, though some experimenting may be necessary. Select according to availability, using either fresh or dried fruit. Try adding various nuts and seeds as well. Makes about two dozen muffins.

3 c. cornmeal
1 1/2 c. w.w. pastry flour
1/4 t. sea salt
1 T. baking powder (optional)
1 1/2 c. fruit or berries, chopped

2-3 T. sesame oil
1 c. barley malt or maple syrup
1 1/2 c. fruit juice
1/2-1 c. nuts, chopped

UNCULTIVATED GARDEN

Combine the dry ingredients, stir in the liquid and sweetener, then add the fruit and mix well. Pour the mixture into well-oiled muffin pans. (Without baking powder, the mixture will not rise, so muffin tins should be filled to the top.) Bake at 325° for 10 minutes, then increase the heat to 375° and continue baking for an additional 15 minutes, or until the muffins are a golden brown.

COUSCOUS CAKE

A very simple, refreshing dessert is made with couscous, the Middle Eastern style of processed wheat. Couscous may be bought in most natural food stores. When I'm in a hurry and want a quick dessert for dinner or a treat, I use this recipe.

1 c. couscous
1/2 c. liquid (fruit juice or water)
1/2 c. barley malt or maple syrup

1 c. wild fruit *
1/2 c. nuts *

Place couscous and liquid in a pan and bring to a boil. Add sweetener and simmer 2-3 minutes. Turn off the heat and stir in the fruit and nuts. Let sit, covered, for at least 15 minutes. Remove from the pan and pat into a casserole dish. Serve plain or with a topping of berries or fruit.

* Strawberries, bramble berries, mulberries, blueberries, or commercial currants or raisins.
* Hickory, walnut, pecan, or sunflower seeds.

GREENS

In the introduction to this section, I mentioned that the edibility of summer's leafy greens varies a lot according to the climate. The list below is fairly reliable throughout most of Northern America's temperate regions.

Normally, the best picking comes from the small, light colored, young leaves at the top of a plant. However, if the plant is growing in areas that have more yin growing conditions, such as rich soil with high moisture content, some older leaves would probably be tender and enjoyable. A cool, wet spell may also bring quick growth and milder flavor to new leaves.

COMMON SUMMER GREENS

Amaranth - top leaves
Carrot - tops, first-year growth
Chickweed - leaves
Comfrey - leaves
Dandelion - leaves
Dock - young leaves
Garlic mustard - leaves, late summer
Garden sorrel - leaves
Grape - tender leaves
Lamb's quarter - top leaves
Mallow - leaves

Milkweed - leaves and pods
Nettle - top
Plantain - tender leaves
Purslane - stalk and leaves
Sheep sorrel - leaves
Thistle - stalks, peeled
Violet - tender leaves
Watercress - leaves
Wood sorrel - leaves, flowers, seeds, pods

In the Spring and Autumn Foraging sections, many suggestions are provided for preparing greens. Please refer to them. Here are a few more.

CREAMY SORREL SOUP

Cream of sorrel soup is popular in Europe. Macrobiotic gourmet and herbalist, Luc Bodin, has eliminated the cream and added tofu to come up with a refreshing similiarity.

1 block tofu, cubed
3" strip kombu
4 c. water
2 c. summer squash, cut in chunks

1 c. wild sheep sorrel, loosely packed *
pinch sea salt
1 t. mirin, or to taste

UNCULTIVATED GARDEN

Steam the tofu for 5 minutes. In a separate pan, bring 4 cups of water to a boil, with the kombu. Remove the kombu, add the squash and tofu, and boil gently until the squash is tender. Puree in a food mill, salt to taste and return to the heat. Chop the sorrel fine and fold it into the simmering liquid. Add mirin to taste and simmer briefly. Garnish with fresh sorrel or parsley.

VARIATION:
- Use cultivated French sorrel, if desired

STEAMED VIOLET AND CABBAGE

Look for a stand of violet plants growing in rich soil. Collect them in early summer when the first crop of summer cabbage matures in the garden, and then again toward autumn when late cabbage is ready for harvest. At both times the violet leaves are most delectable.

2 c. cabbage, sliced thin
1-2 c. violet leaves

violet blossoms
brown rice vinegar or lemon juice

In a steamer rack, steam the cabbage until its color sharpens, then set it aside. Next, steam the violet leaves until they wilt. Toss the greens together with a squeeze of lemon juice or brown rice vinegar, or your favorite dressing. Garnish with violet flowers or another edible flower.

VARIATIONS:
- Substitute leaves of lamb's quarter, young amaranth, young milkweed, nettle, or mild tasting dandelion instead of violet leaves.

SUMMER SALAD

Parboiling summer greens mellows their harsh flavor. So does mixing them with other ingredients. (See Autumn Greens section for another boiled salad recipe.)

1 bunch amaranth tops, bite-size pieces   *3-4 qts. water*
3 med. carrots, cut thin   *pinch sea salt*
1 bunch collard greens, thin strips   *2-4 oz. whole grain noodles*
1/4 head red cabbage, sliced thin

Fill a soup pot 1/2 full of water, add salt and bring to a boil. Use a colander which fits inside the pot. One at a time, place the vegetables in the colander and submerge it in the boiling water until their color sharpens. (Boil greens about 1 minute, cabbage 2 minutes, carrots 3-4 minutes.) Remove and place immediately under cold tap water, drain, and place in a salad bowl. Repeat this procedure until all vegetables are cooked. Start with the mildest tasting vegetable so the water will not be strongly flavored. In this case, the best order is: carrots, collards, cabbage, and lastly, amaranth. Save this cooking water for soup broth or use it to cook the noodles. Meanwhile, boil 2 quarts of water, add the noodles, cook until tender, and drain. Mix the noodles with the vegetables and a favorite dressing or lemon juice.

VARIATIONS:
- Omit the noodles for a refreshing salad with or without dressing.
- Top with toasted sunflower or sesame seeds.
- Use any combination of greens and vegetables which are in season. I recommend violet, lamb's quarter, nettle, mallow, or purslane. Watercress or wood sorrel could be left raw and stirred in at the end while vegetables are still warm.

SUKIYAKI

Sukiyaki is a stove-top Japanese peasant dish which can serve as a substitute for the northern European casserole. It is great in summer for there is no need to heat the oven. I enjoy cooking sukiyaki over the campfire. This adds gourmet flair to any outing. Use whatever is available such as tofu, various kinds of noodles, and a variety of garden or wild produce. Here is one possible combination.

UNCULTIVATED GARDEN 125

1 cake tofu, cut into bite-size pieces
1/2 lb. whole grain noodles, cooked
1 c. wild greens *
1/2 med. head red cabbage, sliced
4 med. carrots, cut on the diagonal (3-4 if wild)
3 c. vegetable stock water
2-4 T. tamari (or good quality soy sauce)

In a large deep skillet or wok, attractively arrange the ingredients in pie-shaped wedges, keeping an eye to color for the most aesthetic arrangement. Slowly add the liquid and bring to a boil. Simmer about 15 minutes until tender, yet crisp. Add tamari and simmer 1-2 minutes more. Serve in the skillet.

* Wild greens: Nettle, violet, lamb's quarter, comfrey (use only 1/2 cup), chickweed, young amaranth, curly dock, young milkweed, first-year carrot, or sea vegetables.

VARIATIONS:
- Other wild roots good in this dish include: parsnip, burdock, salsify, silverweed, day lily, Jerusalem artichoke, and arrowhead.
- Appropriate domestic foods are: parsnip, rutabaga, turnip, daikon or other radish, broccoli, cabbage, cauliflower, brussel sprouts, summer squash, and winter squash.
- Deep-fry the tofu first, then add pieces at the beginning of cooking.
- Cook noodles, or use left-over pasta and add at the beginning of cooking.

ROOTS AND TUBERS

Some roots can be harvested in summer. Their sturdy, downward, yang energy enables us to feel focused and grounded. Edible roots are more abundant for harvest in autumn, winter, and early spring. See these sections for further information and recipes.

COMMON SUMMER ROOTS AND TUBERS

Arrowroot - tuber (thickener)
Burdock - root
Carrot - root
Chicory - root (beverage)
Chufa - tuber
Dandelion - root

Day lily - tuber
Groundnut - tuber
Thistle - root
Salsify - root (late summer)
Wild ginger - rhizome (seasoning and medicinal)

BEANS AND DANDELION ROOT

Mineral-rich dandelion root is cooked with beans to add nutrients and flavor and to cut the gaseous yin effect. Cooked in such a manner, the flavor is scrumptious. This is a basic bean recipe which I utilize constantly when I prepare beans which require a long cooking time (pinto, kidney, navy, black soy, black turtle, soy, lima, or garbanzo beans). The secret to cooking delicious beans is to pressure-cook them with a little kombu seaweed.

1 c. garbanzo beans (or other beans)
4 T. dandelion root, diagonally cut, into 1/2" pieces
3 c. water
4" strip kombu
pinch sea salt

Wash the beans and place them in a pressure cooker with the water and kombu. Boil 10 minutes uncovered. Add dandelion roots. Adjust the pot lid and pressure cook for 50 minutes. Remove from flame. Allow the pressure to come down, add sea salt, and simmer 15 minutes.

VARIATIONS:
- Add 1 cup sliced onion and 1 cup carrots, thinly cut on the diagonal, to the pot at the end of the pressure cooking stage, and simmer 20 minutes.
- Once pressure-cooked, add 1/4 teaspoon (or more) sea salt, soup stock, and vegetables to create bean soup.

MISO SOUP

This recipe is light and refreshing on a cool evening. Miso is a traditional Japanese product rich in vitamin B$_{12}$. It strengthens the blood, stomach, and intestines.

1/c c. day lily tuber (or carrots, sliced) *1 qt. water or stock*
1 sm. burdock root, grated *1 t. white miso (or barley miso)*
2 stalks celery, thinly sliced *1 scallion, chopped fine*

Add the vegetables to cold water and bring to a boil. Simmer 20 minutes. Remove about 1/2 cup stock and puree miso into it to dissolve. Return this to the pan and stir. Sample for flavor; if more miso is desired, add it in the same manner. Turn the flame off and allow the soup to sit covered for 3-4 minutes. Garnish with scallion or wood sorrel. Serve warm or cold.

ADDITIONAL SUGGESTIONS

- Use wild carrot, day lily, arrowroot, ground nut, or salsify in noodle salad, sukiyaki, or casseroles and soup.
- Use a small amount of wild ginger with fish, to flavor stir-fry recipes, or cooked with fruit.

MUSHROOMS

There are many edible summer mushrooms which are relatively easy to identify. Cool, moist environments are conducive to their growth. Please identify mushrooms POSITIVELY before collecting. Many are highly poisonous. For those who value a long and healthy life, avoid sampling to learn if a mushroom tastes edible. In the Spring Foraging section under Mushrooms, further details and recipes, are provided. I choose not to list edible species due to my hope that readers will study mycology in depth. Once educated in the art, many marvelous adventures and meals lie ahead.

LATE SUMMER FORAGING

Earth Element

Late summer is a unique and diverse period and it is important to include a description of it. Food lists and recipes are not included in this section because it would be repetitious and possibly confusing. Please refer to the summer and autumn chapters for recipes which encompass earth element foods. A discussion of seasonal energy characteristics is given here.

Late summer manifests in mid-August at the height of summer's heat and stagnation. The upwardly expanding energy that began in the spring and reached its fullest activity during summer now starts to reverse itself. Atmospheric pressure begins to settle downward in preparation for the period of winter dormancy ahead. At this time the hue of meadows becomes golden, the sky a darker blue, and the breeze takes on a different and somewhat crisper feel. There often occurs a cool and rainy spell at the onset of the earth cycle. With it, leaves begin to fall from a few trees. These subtle changes usually evoke the response, "There's a touch of autumn in the air."

From the onset of this cycle and extending through autumn, there is a strength and hardiness in vegetation which is different from the expansive, yin energy of spring and summer. It makes the wild foods and herbs of these seasons an important resource to be collected, dried, and utilized during winter.

The most abundant harvest of the year, both for cultivated and uncultivated produce, occurs during the earth element period. The ancient Chinese considered late summer as a time of transition as well as a time of maturation and harvest. The sweet flavor is prominent both in fruit and subtly in roots and greens. This flavor is associated with the spleen/pancreas.

It seems odd to many of us to see a chart of five seasons when we are accustomed to four. Each season follows the sun's movement and is marked by the spring and autumn equinox and the summer and winter solstice. Originally the Ancients formulated the Transformation Theory with four seasons, and depicted Earth energy as a continual influence but not a separate stage in the spiral. This model corresponds with the view of Oriental medicine that the spleen/pancreas helps to regulate and balance the entire organism. When the spleen/pancreas is strong, a person feels healthy, emotionally centered, firmly grounded, and in complete control of his or her life. Most people in our modern western society have weakness in this system due to eating an excess of sugar and sweets. Our emotional stability and general health are slipping as a result.

During the two weeks before and after each equinox and solstice, ancient observers noted a strong influence of this earth-type energy which they called doyo. They witnessed that during the transition from one season to another the weather is often erratic and unpredictable, showing patterns of the season which is ending as well as the one approaching. They also noticed these weeks were times of abundant harvest, as if Mother Earth sent forth her strongest energy during these unsettled periods.

The summer to autumn doyo provided the most bountiful harvest of all. This is why the Ancients, in their astute observations of the cycles of nature, eventually gave the late summer doyo its own place on the construct of cyclical transformation. Still important, however, were the remaining three doyo times.

I became intrigued with the doyo concept and for many years paid close attention to weather patterns and the harvest cycles of naturally growing foods. Sure enough, weather certainly is uniquely turbulent or serene during the two weeks prior to and two weeks after each seasonal demarcation. What fascinated me the most was that the majority of wild berries and fruits matured during these four periods. I observed that my spleen/pancreas and lymphatic system tended to be more delicate then, and that this was a beneficial time to focus on healing this system in the manner mentioned in the Five Transformations chapter. It also seemed that I needed to work harder to stay emotionally and physically balanced in the midst of extreme environmental changes around me.

It is important to be aware of these doyo times and adjust our cooking and eating to further enhance stability. Several adjustments support this. We can eat good quality vegetables and sweet-tasting foods instead of rich and sugary sweets. We can also adjust our cooking to reflect the season behind, as well as the one ahead. For example, during the summer/autumn doyo it is wise to slowly add warmth-producing roots and long-cooking recipes such as sturdy stews and hardy soups. If in the late summer we eat a lot of yin fruit and sweets such as ice cream (both of which cool the system) a big discharge of these will naturally come as the system begins to contract (yangize) as a natural adaptation to cooling temperatures. The body on its own accord begins to draw heat inward in an effort to keep internal organs warm and protected against life-threatening cold. Eating too much sugary foods, fruit juice, and commercial fruit in late summer can lead to colds and flu, which are discharges of mucus to cleanse the body. Excess amounts of these foods, especially in the doyo periods, can also lead to a sense of being emotionally unstable and out of control.

For foragers, these doyo periods are prime times to get out and harvest. Between spring and summer, berries are abundant in temperate climates. Late summer and early autumn offer many lush fruits as well as other sweet-tasting foods which can be collected and dried in keeping with the activities of our forbearers. Before and after the winter solstice, the tiny winter fruit of temperate climates is most available and sweet-tasting roots abound.

Late summer foods and recipes are listed in the autumn section.

AUTUMN FORAGING

Metal Element

In autumn, the energy of plants moves downward to roots and tubers, insuring that they will survive during the cold weather ahead. Nutritive power also collects beneath the soil, helping to make roots an important and fortifying food source from autumn through the winter.

Autumn is a strong and invigorating season. Nature's harvest is in full glory. It is a season to hike, forage, and store items safely away for winter. Fruit still abounds; some greens surge again with tender growth; grains, seeds, and nuts mature; roots predominate; and mushrooms may re-emerge after hiding out during the hot, dry summer.

Pungent flavor (as discussed in the Five Transformations section) manifests in various autumn plants, particularly in certain edible roots. This flavor, and the corresponding aspects it represents, helps disperse internal stagnation which also tends to settle downward to the intestines in autumn. Remember that the lungs and large intestine are complimentary organs. During this period of metal element energy, mucus often collects in both organs. It got there because we ate too much fruit and fruit juice, ice cream and dairy products, candy and sodas, and mucus-producing baked items such as bread, cookies, or crackers. As the thermometer drops, our systems voluntarily begin to contract. The body needs to become more yang for winter in order to stay warm. When this internal switching starts, we often get a cold, bronchial problem, or flu. September and October are the times people catch colds because the body is shedding excess yin. The system is cleansing. Pungent-tasting roots such as horseradish, ginger, toothwort, and wild radish help the cleansing. These roots and tubers, along with lotus root, help discharge mucus from the lungs and disperse stagnation in the intestines. (Lotus root resembles a lung in its internal composition. The

Doctrine of Signatures reminds us of its effect. The other roots mentioned look somewhat like intestines.) September through November annually provides a good time to work on healing any weakness or stagnation in the lungs and large intestine.

Quite often the season brings variable weather and many warm days. Beware. It is important to follow environmental cues and slowly adjust our cooking so we can harmonize. For example, September may be intermittently hot. To adjust to the expected cool weather ahead, we can gradually add more roots, nuts, seeds, and grains and longer-cooked foods, including hearty soups and stews on cool days. We may continue to eat raw salads, steamed greens, and light cooking, if the climate dictates. It is helpful to eat cooked fruit instead of raw. Yang heat balances yin sweet. As the temperature continues to drop, we may add more heat to food by cooking, for example, baked casseroles, pressure-cooked grain, and various preparations provided in the recipes below. Furthermore, we may reduce consumption of raw fruit, juice, sweets, and raw foods, and cut back on light cooking styles. If we allow the climate and naturally occurring produce to act as a guide, we may slowly acclimatize to the change.

Native people who lived close to the land worked diligently in autumn to collect and preserve food and fuel. We can too, if we are interested in staying vibrant and healthy when the snow flies.

ROOTS, TUBERS, RHIZOMES

Numerous varieties of roots, tubers, and some rhizomes can be dug during September, October, November, and later if the ground is not frozen. To stretch the harvest time, try covering large roots such as wild parsnip or burdock with about a foot of straw or leaf mulch. Even in very cold climates this protective layer, coupled with snow, will protect the ground below from freezing. The mulch can easily be lifted later so that roots can be dug freely all winter. I will mark patches of burdock and other roots with a stake so they are easy to find. Usually I find locations in or around the garden. This way I can harvest wild and cultivated roots rather quickly on warm winter days. For the most part, I go ahead and dig in late autumn, then store many roots in boxes of sand or dirt in a root cellar or enclosed porch where they may last until February or March. The ground has thawed by then and I can dig some fresh. A few go into the refrigerator for short-term storage.

For long-term preservation, roots can be grated or shaved, then dried and stored in air-tight containers for later use in soups, stews, sukiyaki, casseroles, with grain, or in other recipes. Allow at least 30 minutes for them to soak in water and re-constitute.

When we eat roots, their inwardly-directed yang energy stimulates our orthosympathetic nervous system which works to pull heat inward and contain it deep inside. In this manner, vital organs are protected from extreme cold. The function of the plant pulling its energy downward to survive likewise helps our system to do the same.

Ancient Orientals viewed the intestines as comparable to the roots of plants. Both intestines and roots absorb food, and the intestinal region or "hara" is viewed as the point of internal balance and centering. Many martial arts direct students to focus all their attention on the hara, in order to feel "grounded" deep within, then to direct all movement from this area. Eating root vegetables, wild and domestic, strengthens the hara. Consumption of uncultivated roots, in particular, generates a focusing or grounding force. With their help we can feel very strong and at one with the flow of the universe.

When roots are long-cooked over wood or gas heat, they are further yangized and strengthened. Thus they provide a virtual powerhouse of energy and warmth for our benefit. Eating even a small amount of wild roots or tubers cooked in this manner will help us focus on a task and see it through to completion.

Styles of cooking suitable for autumn (or winter) preparation of roots, tubers, and rhizomes include nishime (waterless cooking), saute, baking (including casseroles), stews, thick soups, pressure-cooking with grains, and tempura (vegetables deep-fried in batter).

COMMON AUTUMN ROOTS AND TUBERS

American lotus - tuber
Arrowhead - tuber
Burdock - root, first year
Calamus - root
Cattail - root
Chicory - root
Dandelion - tuber
Day lily - root
Evening primrose - root *
Great bulrush - tuber
Jerusalem artichoke - tuber
Marshmallow - root
Prairie turnip - tuber

Salsify - root
Sassafrass tree - root
Silverweed - root
Toothwort - root
Thistle - root
Wild carrot - root
Wild ginger - rhizome
Wild leek - bulbs
Wild onion family - bulbs *
Wild parsnip - root
Wild radish - root
Yellow pond lily - tuber

☞ * Evening primrose is fairly bitter tasting. To mellow, marinate it in a 1:1 ratio of tamari, or soy sauce, and water for one hour, then add a small amount to stew or other recipe.
* Wild onion - somewhat resembles death camas; be certain onion aroma is present.

NISHIME

The term "nishime" is Japanese and means waterless cooking. In this recipe a very small amount of liquid is used. The secret to making this dish wonderful and subtly sweet-tasting is to use a strip of kombu seaweed and a cast iron skillet. The kombu adds flavor and provides nutrients including calcium and iron. If kombu is unobtainable, use dandelion root instead. Nishime-style cooking of roots strengthens the intestines and purifies the blood. This basic suggestion can be varied to utilize most root vegetables and allows for dozens of combinations.

UNCULTIVATED GARDEN

1 5-7" strip kombu seaweed, soaked 15 minutes and cut into 1" squares
2 large carrots (domestic), cut into 2" chunks
2-3 turnips, cut into 2" chunks
2 onions, quartered
1/2 c. wild burdock root, cut into 1/2" pieces
2-3 wild parsnip roots, cut into 1-2" pieces
pinch of sea salt
few drops of tamari (if desired)

In a heavy pot, spread kombu strips across the bottom and cover them with water (about 1/2 cup). Layer the roots in the pot, beginning with the most yin so its flavor lifts upward and weds with the condensing flavor of the more yang roots. In this case, start with the onions, followed by the turnip, carrot, parsnip, and burdock. Add a pinch of sea salt. Cover the skillet or pot and place on a high flame until it comes to high steam. Lower flame and simmer peacefully 15-20 minutes; add water if necessary. When the roots are tender, add a few drops of tamari if desired. Cover and simmer 2-5 minutes longer. Remove the lid and serve it right from the skillet.

VARIATIONS:
- Other wild roots which are especially nice in the recipe include: lotus, bulrush, salsify, carrot, onion, silverweed, and Jerusalem artichoke.
- Other domestic vegetables work well too, such as rutabaga, parsnip, or carrot. Also try brussel sprouts, cabbage wedges, broccoli, cauliflower, and pieces of winter squash. All are delicious. Add these on top after the roots have cooked 10 minutes.

FRIED RICE

The following offers a simple preparation which can be a one-dish meal using fresh or left-over rice, and various combinations of ingredients. This basic recipe can be varied literally hundreds of ways.

2 c. cooked brown rice
2 c. Jerusalem artichoke, diced
4-6 c. wild carrots, diced
1 sm. bunch chives, finely chopped
1 T. sunflower seeds, toasted
1/2 t. oil
1/2 t. tamari or soy sauce
1/2 c. water

Brush oil on bottom of a heavy skillet or wok and heat. Add the parsnip and carrots; then saute 2-3 minutes, stirring continuously. Add rice and saute another 3-4 minutes. Add tamari to the water and pour this over the mixture. Cover and simmer on low heat for 5 minutes or until the ingredients are tender. Add chives and sunflower seeds, then serve.

VARIATIONS:
- Slice a small amount of ginger root and saute in oil for 3-4 minutes, then remove the root. Mince 1 teaspoon of it and add back with tamari and water.
- Experiment with other wild roots (except maybe evening primrose, horseradish, sassafras, or chicory).
- Select from a large variety of domestic vegetables.
- Add tofu or cooked tempeh for extra protein.

BAKED PARSNIPS

Baking offers a simple way to add more energy to root vegetables. I like to bake in a Dutch oven over campfire coals. When back-packing, I cook them directly in the coals wrapped tightly in aluminum foil. Wild root vegetable dishes are so potent when cooked on wood heat that a small bowl is satisfying, yet offers fuel to hike many miles.

VEGETABLES:
4-6 wild parsnips, long pieces
1/4 c. water

SAUCE:
1 T. lemon juice
1 T. white miso
2 T. water

Arrange parsnips in a small casserole dish. Add water or sauce. Cover and bake for 35-45 minutes at 350° or until soft. (If using aluminum foil over coals, omit the lemon. The acid reacts adversely with the aluminum.)

VARIATIONS:
- Most wild roots are flavorful when baked. Bitter types such as dandelion, chicory, burdock, or evening primrose are best chopped fine. Add a small amount to domestic or wild vegetables, and include them as an addition to a grain, noodle, or vegetable casserole recipe. If you experiment by using small amounts of wild roots you will become familiar with their flavor.

UNCULTIVATED GARDEN

AUTUMN STEW

Stew and thick soup seem to really satisfy in autumn, especially when large chunks of root vegetables are used. Use domestic root vegetables and supplement with wild. Suitable wild ingredients include: burdock, parsnip, wild carrot, salsify, Jerusalem artichoke, onion, lotus, marsh mallow, arrowroot, prairie turnip, silverweed, or dandelion. Evening primrose or chicory can also be used in small amounts. Here's one possible combination:

3 med. commercial carrots, cut into 2" chunks
3 med. turnips, quartered
2-3 wild or domestic parnips, cut into 2" chunks
2 med. onions, quartered
6" piece burdock root, 1/2" chunks

3 lotus roots, or 4-5 Jerusalem artichokes, sliced (optional)
1 t. dark sesame oil
4 T. flour (rice, w.w. or other)
1 T. mugi miso
2 c. water or stock

Heat oil in a Dutch oven or heavy pot. Add the onions and saute 1-2 minutes. Add other vegetables and saute 3-4 minutes. Add stock or water and bring to a boil. Reduce heat, and slow-simmer for at least 1 hour, preferably longer. Stir the flour into 1/2 cup of water to make a white sauce, add miso and puree. Add this blend to the stew and stir. Let simmer for 5 more minutes to thicken, but avoid boiling. Serve hot. If miso is unavailable, season with tamari or add sea salt at the beginning of the simmering process.

VARIATIONS:
- Chop wild greens and add them during the final 5-6 minutes of cooking.
- Instead of flour, thicken with arrowroot powder or kuzu.

BROWN RICE, BURDOCK, AND DRIED TOFU

Pressure-cooking rice (or other grains) helps them to strengthen our overall condition. Organic short grain brown rice is especially delicious. Brown rice has metal energy. Between this and the burdock, the following recipe is particularly helpful for intestines and/or prostate.

2 c. short grain brown rice *2 1/2 c. water*
4-6" piece burdock root, diced *pinch sea salt*
2 cakes dried tofu

Wash rice and place it in a pressure cooker. Scrub the burdock root and cut it diagonally into 1/2" long logs. Soak the dried tofu pieces for 10 minutes, then cut them into 1" pieces. Add the burdock and dried tofu to the rice. Cover with 2 1/2 cups water and bring to a boil. Add a pinch of salt, cover, and bring to pressure. Cook 50 minutes, then remove from the flame and allow the pressure to come down slowly and naturally.

WHOLE WHEAT BERRIES AND WILD PARSNIP

The sweet flavor of the wheat and parsnip makes them effective to stimulate the spleen, pancreas, and lymphatic system.

2 c. soft spring wheat *3 c. water*
1 c. wild parsnip, cut into 1" pieces *pinch of sea salt*

Wash the wheat and allow it to soak in water for 2-4 hours. Place in a pressure cooker with the parsnip. Bring to a boil and add salt. Cover and allow to come to full pressure. Reduce the heat and cook for 75 minutes on low pressure. Remove from the flame and the allow pressure to come down slowly.

VARIATIONS:
- If unable to use a pressure cooker, double the amount of water and simmer 5-8 hours or cook overnight on low heat. You might try it on a wood stove for a hot, ready-to-eat breakfast cereal.

UNCULTIVATED GARDEN

- Add currants or raisins at the beginning for a pleasant breakfast cereal. Or add winter squash, cut in 1" chunks.
- If using winter wheat instead of spring wheat, soak overnight and pressure cook 90 minutes on low pressure, or simmer for 6-8 hours after doubling the amount of water.

ADDITIONAL SUGGESTIONS

- The dispersive nature of the pungent roots helps the body break up oil and fat deposits. If they are grated and eaten with deep-fried or other oily foods, their pungent essence allows the liver to digest the oil more efficiently.
- Grate wild ginger and use it as a condiment for soup, or to season baked fish, casseroles, sauteed dishes, and desserts. The flavor is distinctive and earthy, much different than its commercial Asian counterpart.
- Wild horseradish root can be grated for a potent, dispersive condiment.

GREENS

Around the time of the autumn equinox, a cold front often will bring early frost and/or thunderstorms. Garden vegetables may need to be covered to prevent early crop loss, but to lovers of wild greens, the cold snap is welcome. Many greens such as nettle, wild lettuce, poke, mustard family, dock, and comfrey begin a short but mighty autumn growing cycle. Other greens such as violet, dandelion, and plantain usually get a surge of growth as cool, damp weather persists. Many of these species have large tender leaves again, much like in the spring. But the vegetation of autumn is different than spring growth for the same variety of plant. For example, fall greens manifest a subtle, sweet or pungent flavor as opposed to the sour springtime taste.

Autumn's hearty, durable greens are wonderful to collect and dry for winter. Store them in air-tight glass jars. They last better if they are stored in whole leaf form rather than powdered, as we often see in stores. More nutrition and ki is retained.

I rely on dried greens almost daily during January, February, and March. It is simple to add a tablespoon or so to a pot of tea, or to soup stock, and use this as cooking water for grains, stew, or other dishes.

If you are not able or motivated to collect and dry greens, go to a health food or herb store and purchase bulk supplies of such greens as nettle, dandelion, violet, and others. A half pound of each will likely get a family through the winter. Lazy foraging? Maybe, but the Native Americans say "take what you have and make do." Purchasing dried greens can start you along the wild foods route; every journey begins with the first step.

COMMON AUTUMN GREENS

Dandelion
Docks - curly and broadleaf
Garlic mustard
Lamb's quarter
Nettle
Onion family
Plantain

Poke - young plants only
Purslane
Sorrels - sheep and wood
Violet
Watercress
Wild carrot - 1st-year tops only *
Wild lettuce

☞ * Wild carrot - second year growth, known as Queen Anne's Lace, is usually 2-3 feet tall and poisonous. First year tops are about 4-6 inches tall.
* It is the NEW GROWTH of young plants which is to be gathered. Some plants such as poke or nettle may be 5-8 feet tall by fall. Seek the infant crop, less than one foot high.

CARROT TOP PESTO

Digging carrots in the autumn, you can suddenly find yourself inundated with tops. Anna Bond (macrobiotic cook, gardener, and herbalist) offers this way to preserve some green color for the white months. Anna uses her garden carrot tops and supplements with wild ones. Tops of the first-year wild carrots are more tender than those of domestic carrots, making them delicious in this and other recipes.

1 c. fresh carrot tops, chopped
1/2 c. parsley
1/2 c. olive oil
2 T. umeboshi paste
2-3 cloves garlic, minced
1/2 c. pine nuts or walnuts

Grind the chopped carrot tops and parsley in the blender. Add the remaining ingredients and blend on high speed until the mixture forms a thick paste. Store, tightly sealed, in the refrigerator or freezer.

WILD GREENS SAUTE

Sauteing is an energizing style of cooking. Have a sauteed meal before going out to chop wood. Use an entire plant, root and top, for a dynamic interplay of yin and yang energies which helps bring you to a centered state. This is needs to be experienced to be understood.

1 med. onion, cut in half moons
2 sm. turnips, cut in wedges
1 bunch turnip greens, sliced
1 bunch nettles (new growth), chopped
1 dandelion plant, root and greens, minced
dark sesame oil or other

In a wok or cast iron skillet, heat a few drops of oil and saute the onions and dandelion root 1-2 minutes. Add turnip root and saute them all together 4-5 minutes. Add greens and saute 3-4 minutes. Add a few drops of tamari to 2 tablespoon water and pour this over the greens. Stir, cover, and steam 2-4 minutes. Serve hot with toasted sesame seeds, if desired.

VARIATION:
- Use other combinations of domestic or wild greens and roots.

WATERCRESS, KALE, AND CABBAGE

Another style of saute uses water, with or without oil and is also quite vitalizing. This recipe utilizes autumn garden produce and food from the stream. The foraging is simple for me because of the stream which flows through our cloistered mountain valley. I collect cress from the spring beside the little Methodist Church and call it "holy" cress because it grows at the outdoor chapel which I so dearly love. Since I've been collecting and praising it, the patch has continually grown much larger and fuller.

1/4 c. water
1/4 t. sesame oil, if desired
1/4 small head cabbage, thinly sliced
1/2 bunch kale, thinly sliced

1 c. watercress, cleaned, roots removed, and cut in 2" pieces
tamari or soy sauce, to taste

In a heavy skillet or wok, heat water and oil. Add cabbage and simmer, stirring occasionally. Cook 3-5 minutes, stir in kale, cover and simmer another 5 minutes, or until the color of both greens sharpens and they are tender. Add tamari and simmer 1 minute. Turn off the flame and make a crater in the center of the greens. Place watercress in the crater, cover, and let the pan sit 3-5 minutes. (Watercress is mostly water. If cooked too long it will shrink down to almost nothing.)

VARIATIONS:
- Use various wild greens such as dock instead of kale, or use other domestic greens.
- Top with toasted sunflower seeds or dressing.

DANDELION ONION TEMPURA

While visiting the remote Vermont farm of Luc Bodin and Anna Bond, I was treated to the following recipe and wanted to include it for others to savour. Anna used onion and briefly rehydrated dulse together in tempura, too. It was delicious and unique.

1 part rice flour
2 parts whole wheat pastry flour
1 t. (heaping) arrowroot flour
pinch sea salt
cold water

safflower or sesame oil
tender dandelion greens
onions

Prepare the batter by mixing the dry ingredients and adding enough ice-cold water to make a thin pancake mixture. (If doing a large amount of tempura, keep ice cubes in the batter, since the crispness of the tempura depends on the temperature differential between the cold batter and the hot oil.) Use the batter soon after making it.

Slice the onions into thin half-moon slivers and chop the dandelion finely. Stir these into the batter without excess agitation. Drop teaspoon-sized clumps of vegetable-batter mixture into the hot oil with long chopsticks. Turn once and remove when golden. Drain on brown paper bags or paper towels. Serve with a dip made of tamari and grated horseradish.

VARIATION:
- Instead of onion use an equal amount of dulse and dandelion leaves. Separate the dried dulse into small pieces and proceed as above.

MILLET SOUP

Fresh greens add color and richness to soups and stews.

1/3 c. millet, rinsed well
1/2 c. wild onion (1 c. domestic), diced
1 c. winter squash (butternut, hubbard, hokkaido, buttercup, acorn, sweet mamma, etc.) cut into 1" cubes

1 c. young nettle leaves, cut small
4 c. water or vegetable stock
2 pinches sea salt
tamari or miso to taste
1 T. chives, minced

In a cooking pot, layer the onion and squash, then spread the millet evenly on top. Gently add water and simmer for 25 minutes, or until the millet softens. Avoid stirring. Add chopped greens atop the millet and simmer 5 minutes longer. Stir and season with tamari or miso to taste. Garnish with chives if desired.

VARIATIONS:
- Use bulgur, corn grits, or oat groats.
- Use other greens such as watercress, violet, wild carrot tops, or dandelion.
- Add diced roots such as wild burdock, parsnip, carrot, or silverweed.
- Add herbs at beginning for extra seasoning. Layer them on the bottom with the onions so their yin nature expands upward to flavor the other ingredients.

AUTUMN BOILED SALAD

Boiled salad is an appropriate all-season dish. It is light and refreshing. Use wild or domestic greens along with various vegetables to create a colorful display. Two possible combinations are: 1) watercress, carrot, celery and red cabbage; or 2) purslane, carrot, and broccoli.

In a cooking pot, place a pinch of sea salt into 6-8 inches of water and bring to a boil. Have 3-5 vegetables sliced and ready. One at a time, place vegetables in a colander and lower it into the boiling water until their color sharpens. Cook the mildest-flavored vegetable first so each will retain its flavor. Remove from the pan, drain, and place in a bowl. Repeat this procedure for each vegetable or green, and save the stock for soup. Serve with a favorite dressing or toasted seeds.

GRAINS

Numerous wild grains ripen and can be harvested in autumn. Collecting them, however, can be tedious. I suggest shaking them into a bag. Many can be winnowed free of their surrounding chaff by rubbing them between the hands and blowing away the casing. This was children's work in many traditional cultures, and was done a little at a time during cold weather. I can imagine the children winnowing seeds as some old grandfather entertained them with a story. We have TV today, not as quaint, but it may offer diversion during the task. Store the precious few grains which are gleaned in an air-tight glass jar for winter use. Make sure they are dry first or they will get moldy. The life force of grains is tremendous. Properly stored, grain can be preserved hundreds of years and remain viable. (I am told that grain was found in King Tut's tomb and it was still able to grow!)

The amount of vital ki provided in grains is remarkable. Each tiny grain contains within it the essence of a new life; each is holds the responsibility for the continuation of its species. According to Oriental teachings, the appearance of humans and cereal grains coincided on the Earth. Grain is brain food. It activates the mind to higher levels of perception and wholistic thought. Round or symmetrical in shape, grains and seeds represent the final product of the mother plant's growth, and from yang to yin to yang again, they are the end and the beginning. When we eat them, a transformation occurs in our linear kind of thinking and we perceive nature as an ever-changing flow of cycles which spiral into an intricate dance.

Wild grains are potent. Add 1-2 teaspoons to a cup of commercial whole grain as a supplement. Use in porridges, soups, and stews, or add to flour to use in bread or muffin recipes.

COMMON AUTUMN GRAINS AND SEEDS

Amaranth
Chufa (yellow nut grass)
Dock
Great bulrush
Large cane

Reed (Phragmites)
Sunflower
Wild millet *
Wild rice *

☞ * Sometimes a pink or purplish ergot fungus will replace the seeds of wild millet or rice. It is highly poisonous. When hardened, it can assume the same size and shape of the grain although it is often larger and shows obvious deformity. Please use your all-important common sense. If ergot is present, collect elsewhere. The purple color indicates strong yin.

WILD RICE WITH HAZELNUTS AND BLUEBERRIES

Wild rice can be collected in northern wetlands or purchased commercially. Either way, this recipe requires some serious dedication and may therefore be saved for a very special occasion.

2 c. wild rice, washed
4 c. water
2 onions, diced

1 c. dried blueberries (or 1 1/2 c. fresh)
1 c. dried hazelnuts, shelled and chopped

In a kettle, place the rice atop a base layer onions. Gently add water down the side of the pot and bring to a boil. Add a pinch of sea salt, and simmer 40 minutes or until most of the water is absorbed. Add the hazelnuts and dried blueberries. Cover and simmer 5 minutes more. Remove from flame, stir and let sit, covered, for 5 minutes. Serve hot.

THANKSGIVING STUFFED SQUASH

Another festive use of wild rice is to include it in a stuffing for chicken, turkey, or mock turkey. For vegetarians who miss the big bird, try the following. I am usually able to locate green or blue hubbard squash which resembles a turkey in size and shape. This is the center of our Thanksgiving and Christmas dinners and is a delightful replacement.

1 large winter squash or pumpkin, seeds removed
2 c. brown rice
2 c. wild rice (or other wild grain)
3/4 c. burdock root, diced
1 c. puffball or other edible mushrooms, sliced

2 large onions, diced (or bunch wild chives)
1/2 c. sunflower seeds, roasted in skillet
2 stalks celery, diced
1/2 t. oil (dark sesame or other)
5 c. water

Wash rice and place in pressure cooker along with burdock. Cover with the water and bring to a boil. Add a pinch of sea salt, cover, and bring to pressure. Cook 50 minutes, then remove from the flame and allow the pressure to come down slowly and naturally. If there's no pressure cooker handy, slowly boil the rice with 8 cups water and simmer 50 minutes, undisturbed. Meanwhile, spread oil on the bottom of a heavy skillet or wok, heat, and saute the onions for 2 minutes. Add the celery and mushrooms, then saute 4-5 minutes or until soft. Mix with the prepared rice. Cut the top off the squash, remove the seeds and fill it with the rice mixture. Replace the top, place the whole masterpiece in a casserole dish with 1/2" water and bake at 350° for approximately 1 hour. Serve on a big platter surrounded by lightly boiled greens and vegetables such as kale, turnip, and carrots.

PORRIDGE

I savor grains and vegetables cooked together as porridge. Such a concoction activates species memories inside me of primitive relatives eating simple meals around the campfire. Here is one possible suggestion. Various wild grains can be used.

3 c. wild greens stock
3/4 c. oatmeal flakes
1 t. amaranth grain

1 c. rutabaga, cubed
1/2 c. brussel sprouts, sliced
1-2 t. miso (if desired)

To make the stock, steep 2-3 tablespoon dried nettle, violet leaves, lamb's quarter, amaranth, plantain, or other mild tasting dried green in 3 cups of water. Simmer for 5 minutes; avoid boiling. Remove from flame, steep 15 minutes, and strain. Add amaranth, oats, and rutabaga to the stock and simmer, covered, for 20 minutes on low heat. (Use a flame deflector to avoid scorching.) Add brussel sprouts and simmer 10 minutes more until the sprouts are tender but still bright green. Remove a little broth and puree the miso into it. Stir this into the porridge. Cover. Remove from heat and let sit 2-3 minutes. Serve warm.

VARIATIONS:
- Garnish with watercress sprigs or toasted sunflower seeds.
- Use other vegetables, wild or domestic.
- Instead of using miso add 1/4 teaspoon salt at the beginning.

WHOLE WHEAT BREAD

Autumn is a wonderful season to fill the house with the aroma of baked bread. The use of some wild seeds will add a unique flavor and extra nutrition. Try various edible seeds. Sample a few first to envision whether the flavor will blend well with bread. Most of them taste great.

3 1/2 c. w.w. flour
1 T. active dry yeast
1 c. warm water
4 t. barley malt

1 t. sea salt
3/4-1 c. warm water
1/4 c. sunflower seeds, toasted
1 T. other wild seeds or dried greens

Pour the flour into a large bowl and place in the oven at the lowest temperature for 15 minutes to warm. In a small bowl, sprinkle the yeast over the warm water, add the warm barley malt and stir. Allow this mixture to sit for 5 minutes and add it to the warm flour. Add salt and stir in enough warm water to make a sticky dough. Knead the dough at least 10 minutes. Oil a loaf pan. Put the dough into it, and set it in a warm place to rise for 45 minutes to 1 hour, or until the dough rises slightly over the pan rim. Place into a preheated oven and bake at 400° for 30-40 minutes or until golden brown. Allow the loaf to cool for 10 minutes before removing it from the pan.

NUTS

Autumn brings with it a major harvest of nuts. Rich in oil, nuts help us store up a little extra fatty insulation for cold weather. Nuts are high in protein and thus quite energizing. Their oily quality is expansive and yin. It is best to roast them a bit in the oven or on top of the stove. This way nuts are more digestible, and their oil is easily assimilated into the body. Roasting yangizes the oily yin. Cooking or serving them with a little salt, tamari, or seaweed also helps bring balance for purposes of digestion and assimilation.

Many nuts need to be collected as soon as they fall; squirrels or worms will beat you to the treasure if you dawdle. I often collect every few days when the hickory

UNCULTIVATED GARDEN

or chestnut harvest is at its peak. My elderly neighbor is sly about his hickory harvest. On a sunny afternoon he sits outdoors watching football on TV, and keeping an eye on his hickory trees. When the game is dull, he gathers newly fallen nuts before his friendly squirrels escape with the entire cache. Acorn, hickory, chestnut, pecan, and others are likely to fall en masse after a strong wind storm. I like to wait for this. These storms seem to hit each year about nut harvesting time. The following morning the squirrels and I are busy stocking up.

Nuts should be shelled, dried, and stored in air-tight containers for optimal results. By spring or summer bugs may invade. To help prevent this situation, put the entire jar into the freezer overnight, before the bugs become active.

COMMON AUTUMN NUTS

Acorn - white oak family
Beech
Black walnut
Butternut
Chestnut *

Chinquapin
Hazelnut
Hickory
Pecan
Pinon

☛ * Chestnut - There is a toxic horse chestnut. The nut itself closely resembles that of the delicious American chestnut, but everything else about the tree and nut housing is different. The edible American chestnut grows, or grew, in the Eastern U.S. Due to a blight, most trees are now fruitless sprouts from the old stumps. Trees are small otherwise, about 30 feet tall. Leaves are large, spear-shaped, coarsely toothed, and hairless. Stiff, prickly husks contain hundreds of tiny spines. Inside this husk are 2 or 3 flattened seeds, each about 1-inch across. Leaves of the toxic horse chestnut look completely different. They are primarily compound and have 5-7 elliptical or lance-shaped leaflets. The husks are also different, green capsules with short spines which are much more widely separated.

ACORN GRIDDLE CAKES

Griddle cakes are always fun. The following is a unique treat. Acorns must be blanched, shells and husks removed, then boiled for several hours. Every 10 minutes, pour off the cooking water and add fresh water. When the flavor is enjoyable, dry roast them in an oven at 350° until completely dry. Store them in glass jars. Grind the nuts to make flour and save enough for later use in muffins or more griddle cakes. It's a lot of work, but an adventure to try!

1 t. toasted sesame oil
3 T. wild leeks or chives, chopped
1 c. cornmeal
1 c. acorn flour
1/4 c. pastry or whole wheat flour

1/4 t. sea salt
1 t. baking powder (optional)
1 c. milk or plain soy milk
1/2 t. cayenne pepper sauce or hot pepper sauce (to taste)

Add 1/2 teaspoon dark sesame oil to a skillet, heat over a medium flame, and saute leeks or chives 2-3 minutes. Sift together the cornmeal, acorn flour, pastry flour, salt, and baking powder. Add soy milk and onions to the dry ingredients and stir well. Add hot sauce to taste, and continue stirring until the batter is well mixed; avoid over-stirring. Coat a pancake griddle or heavy skillet with the remaining 1/2 teaspoon oil and turn the heat to medium. Spoon the batter onto the hot griddle and cook until bubbles begin to break. Turn the hot cake and cook until the second side is golden brown.

This recipe is great at lunch or dinner served with beans, especially pinto beans cooked with dandelion root.

VARIATION:
- Instead of onions and hot sauce, use 1/2 cup chopped cranberries and top with applesauce or maple syrup.

BAKED RICE AND CHESTNUTS

This is a very invigorating, cold weather, high protein preparation. It is heat producing because of the long baking time. Try other nuts in the recipe. Walnuts, hickory, and pinon are delicious.

UNCULTIVATED GARDEN

2 c. short or medium grain brown rice, rinsed
4 c. boiling water
1/4 t. sea salt
3/4 c. chestnuts

Puncture chestnuts with a knife to make a small "x" on the shell. Rinse the rice and dry roast it in a cast iron or heavy skillet until slightly brown. Meanwhile, blanch the chestnuts in boiling water for 10 minutes, remove the shell and husk, and cut into quarters. In a casserole dish, place the rice, nuts, and sea salt, and cover with boiling water. Bake, covered at 350° for 1 hour. The rice will be light, fluffy, and easy to digest.

VARIATIONS:
- Use 1/2 cup wild rice and 1 1/2 cups brown rice.
- Pressure cook rice and chestnuts together.

FLOURLESS NUT COOKIES

These cookies are my favorite because they are quick and simple to make and because I like the not-too-sweet taste. This nutritious snack is made without sugar or honey. It uses barley malt, which is made from whole barley, is absorbed slowly into the blood stream, and has a gentle effect on blood sugar levels. Most any kind of nut is yummy. Along with the applesauce I use various dried or fresh fruits such as persimmon, cranberries, dried peaches, and pears.

3 c. rolled oats
4 apples (or 1 c. applesauce)
1/2 c. raisins, currants, or other
2-6 T. barley malt
1/2 c. hickory nuts (or other), chopped
1/2 t. cinnamon (or spicebush twigs)

Core the apples, quarter and puree them in a blender with a little water (or juice). Combine all the ingredients and allow the mixture to sit 15 minutes. Meanwhile, preheat the oven to 350°. Roll the batter into firm balls, flatten them, and bake 20 minutes or until golden brown on both top and bottom. Makes 1 dozen.

VARIATION:
- Use maple syrup instead of barley malt.

WINTER SQUASH AND NUT DESSERT

Squash strengthens the spleen/pancreas function and so do nuts when eaten in moderation.

1 large butternut (or other sweet winter squash)
1/2 c. currants or raisins

1/2 c. hickory nuts, walnuts, pecans or other
1 T. barley malt

Remove the squash seeds, cut the squash into chunks and boil them in a small amount of water, along with the currants. When soft, mash the squash. Add nuts and barley malt, then simmer 5 minutes. For extra flavor, oven-roast the nuts at 350° for about 10 minutes. Serve warm.

VARIATIONS:
- Kuzu or arrowroot powder can be added to thicken.
- Use as pie filling with your favorite crust, adding cinnamon and nutmeg to taste.

FRUIT

During the transition from autumn to winter, large, sweet, and juicy yin fruit, such as pawpaw and apples, give way to more condensed yang varieties such as cranberries or rose hips.

Fruit in general is rich in vitamins A, B_2, and C and can easily be dried in a dehydrator, above a wood stove, or outdoors on netting. (See Summer Foraging for details.) Dry below 165°F to retain the flavor and vitamins. To reconstitute, soak in water or juice. Store enough for winter and spring. In cold weather it is wise to eat fruit and berries cooked, to yangize them.

UNCULTIVATED GARDEN

COMMON AUTUMN FRUITS AND BERRIES

American hackberry	Cranberry	Rose hips
Apple	Elderberry	Sandhill plum
Barberry	Grape *	Sumac
Black cherry	Ground cherry	Wild currant
Black crowberry	Hawthorn	Wild raisin
Blueberry	Mountain ash	Wintergreen
Chokecherry	Pawpaw	
Crabapple	Persimmon	

☞ * Wild grape somewhat resembles the poisonous moonseed fruit. Pay attention when collecting. Grapes have several small seeds inside, but moonseed has one large, crescent-shaped seed. Grape vines have small tendrils which attach the grape vine to nearby plants or objects. Moonseed vines, on the other hand, wind themselves entirely around an object.

* Check resource books for which fruits are commonly found in your region and in which habitat each thrives.
* Refer to the Summer section for more fruit recipes.

MEATLESS PEMMICAN

American Indians preserved fruit, nuts, grain, and seeds by making jerky or pemmican. Traditionally, these were shredded with bear, buffalo, or deer meat. This is a meatless recipe.

1/2 c. currants or raisins
1/2 c. sunflower or sesame seeds
1/2 c. hickory nuts
1/2 c. dried apples or other fruit

1/2 c. dried squash or pumpkin
1 c. acorn (or corn) meal
1/3 c. barley malt

Leach the bitterness from white oak acorns as explained in the Acorn Griddle Cake recipe earlier. (Burr oak is less bitter.) Grind, then roast in the oven at 300° on a cookie sheet for 15-30 minutes, or until dry. At the same time, roast the seeds and nuts until golden. Combine all the ingredients except the sweetener. Grind in a food mill or chop fine with a knife. Add the barley malt. Divide into small handfuls and form into patties. Store in a cool place. This is a yummy autumn treat, great for children.

VARIATION:
- Experiment with various fruits and nuts.

APPLE-GRAPE COMPOTE

A simple dessert is shown here and can be varied to utilize numerous seasonal fruits, berries, and nuts. Commercially processed kuzu root thickens and makes the dish more yang and strengthening. Wild grape varieties vary tremendously, and many varieties of commercial grapes are found growing wild. Wild apples usually mean apple trees from old farmsteads. They are small, but energizing.

6 apples, cut into bite-size chunks
1 bunch purple grapes, seeds removed
2 c. water or juice
6" spicebush twig or 1/2 t. cinnamon
pinch sea salt
2 T.(heaping) commercial kuzu root, arrowroot powder, or cornstarch
1/4 c. walnuts (optional)

In a saucepan, simmer the first 5 ingredients for 15 minutes or until cooked. Dissolve kuzu in 1/4 cup cool tap water and add it to the fruit mixture. Stir constantly and allow to cook until the kuzu becomes clear and a thick sauce develops. Spread the walnuts on a cookie sheet and bake at 300° for 5-7 minutes until they turn golden. Be careful for they scorch easily. Chop them and add to fruit at end of cooking time. Serve warm. Add additional sweetener, if desired.

PERSIMMON BUTTER

Persimmons have a fruity, brown sugar flavor. They taste good atop muffins or pancakes when cooked for persimmon butter. Use persimmons in muffins, quick bread, or pudding recipes as well.

Rinse 2 lbs. persimmons and remove stems and seeds. Place in a heavy pot with a little water or apple juice. Simmer, covered, on a low flame for 1 hour. Mash or run through an old-fashioned potato ricer to remove the seeds.

UNCULTIVATED GARDEN

VARIATION:
- Combine with other fruit such as apples or pears to cut the sugary flavor.

FRUIT BARS

2 c. fruit juice or water
1/2 t. sea salt
2 c. wild fruit, chopped *
1 c. oat flakes
1/4 c. oil

1 c. corn meal
1 c. w.w. pastry flour
1 c. wheat germ or finely ground wheat
1 c. sesame seed, toasted

Soak the first four ingredients together for 1/2 hour. Stir in oil, then add the remaining ingredients. Allow to stand for 1/2 hour and pour about 1" deep into a greased baking dish. Bake at 375° for 15 minutes. Remove, cut, and bake 15-20 minutes longer. They will be crumbly when cooked.

VARIATION:
- Use wild fruit such as blueberries, plums, persimmon, pawpaw, raisins or apples. Other autumn fruit (such as elderberry or chokecherry) can be simmered and pressed through a sieve to make pulp, then added in a small ratio.

WILD FRUIT SYRUP AND JELLY

2 lb. blueberries or sandhill plum, cleaned *
3 bags mu tea (optional)

10 c. water or apple cider
1/2 t. sea salt

In a large, heavy-bottom sauce pan, simmer mu tea bags in liquid to a full-bodied flavor. Remove tea bags, add fruit and bring to a boil. Lower the flame, add sea salt, cover the pan, and simmer for 2 hours, stirring occasionally. Strain syrup and reserve the liquid. (Leftover pulp may be used in cake or cookie batter). Return the liquid to the pan and boil down to desired sweetness.

For thicker syrup, dissolve 2 tablespoon arrowroot flour in a small amount of syrup, return to pan, and simmer for several minutes, until the syrup is clear and thick. Use as a fruit jelly.

VARIATION:
* Experiment with using other fruit and fruit combinations.

JERUSALEM ARTICHOKE-RAMP SAUTE

If you have ever planted Jerusalem artichokes and watched them take over the garden, you will be happy to find more ways to use them.

2 c. Jerusalem artichokes, sliced
1 c. wild ramps, thinly sliced
1 c. kombu cooking stock

1 t. dark sesame oil
tamari to taste

In a heavy skillet, saute J. artichokes in oil on a high flame, add kombu broth, lower flame, cover, and continue cooking until tender but not to the point of falling apart. Add ramps to the steaming tubers. Saute 1-2 minutes to cook slightly and retain the color. Season with tamari or sea salt.

JERUSALEM ARTICHOKE PICKLES

1 pint tamari
1 pint water
1/2 c. fresh horseradish root, grated
1 1/2 quarts Jerusalem artichokes, sliced thin
1/2 quart Kombu seaweed, soaked and cut into 1" squares

Prepare a pickling brine with good quality tamari and spring or well water. Simmer about 1/2 cup of brine with the grated horseradish for 5 minutes to extract the juices. Strain and allow to cool, then add it back the other brine. Soak the kombu about 30 minutes, cut it into squares, and parboil for twenty minutes. Allow to cool. Mix the artichokes with the kombu. Pack these vegetables loosely into 2 quart canning jars, and fill the jars to the top with the cooled brine. Seal and store in a cool, dark place. Taste in 3 weeks.

ADDITIONAL SUGGESTIONS

- Use pawpaw in place of banana in a favorite banana nut bread recipe.
- For corn meal or other muffins, experiment by adding black cherry, blueberry, cranberry, grape, ground cherry, pawpaw, persimmon, rose hip pulp (cooked and strained), plum, wild currant, or raisin. Crabapple and chokecherry have a strong flavor. They can be used in small amounts with extra sweetener and are nice mixed with apples.
- In oatmeal cookies, try using persimmon, pawpaw, ground cherry, and other autumn fruits.
- Most of the fruit recipes listed in this book can be varied to include autumn fruits.

WINTER FORAGING

Water Element

Yes, foraging is possible in winter, even in cold northern regions where a thick blanket of snow covers the ground. Of course, you will find a lot more if there is no snow. The foods which thrive are extremely nutritious. Watercress is a hardy winter survivor. It contains 4,900 I.U. of vitamin A per 3 1/2 ounces, 79 mg of vitamin C, 151 mg of calcium, and 2.2 grams of protein. Even a few sprigs in soup add tremendous nutrition and ki to a winter meal. Vegetation is sparse in winter, but potent.

A few green treasures are always available in snowy climates. This may only be pine needles and maybe a few clusters of chives peeking through the white blanket, but that's just enough for evergreen tea or soup broth, and a garnish of minced chives.

During winter we must rely heavily on food which was collected earlier. But brisk wintertime foraging treks are great. Fresh air, sunshine, and exercise all nourish the forager tremendously. So what if only meager resources are found; there's a lot more to foraging than gathering food. The hunt provides a good reason to get outdoors and appreciate the beauty of a serene winter landscape. A brisk hike gets your ki moving and helps work up a justifiable appetite.

If winter gathering is a problem, or if you run out of stored items, it is often possible to buy a variety of dried greens and roots. Find a health food store or food co-op which carries bulk herbs. Often they will have (or can order) nettle, violet, plantain, lamb's quarter leaves, burdock root, dandelion root, chicory root, and many medicinal herbs. Try and get good quality stock.

The Five Transformations Theory indicates that many winter plants have a mineral or salty flavor. This taste is a clue to the powerful yang tendencies which have warming quality, and which enhance health and vitality. The color black also predominates. For example, sea vegetables manifest both a salty/mineral flavor, and a blackish color. Rich in vitamins and minerals, they are important winter vegetables. Once dried, seaweed maintains its high nutrition for many years. We are fortunate in the U.S. to be able to purchase dried sea vegetables such as kelp and kombu, dulse, nori, arame, hiziki, wakame, and alaria. Many seaweeds are imported, but mail order is possible from Maine.[10]

Oriental medicine practitioners saw winter as a time to strengthen fluid-regulating organs such as the kidneys and bladder. Water plants assist in this. Sea vegetables, watercress, and water tubers are highly beneficial winter fare which keeps these organs in good condition.

GREENS

The resources listed below are likely to be found in temperate climates all winter - even below the snow. Realistically, the deep winter months offer slim pickings, so plan ahead and turn to dried supplements.

COMMON WINTER GREENS

Chives
Dandelion
Garlic mustard
Eastern hemlock tree-needles *

White pine tree-needles *
Watercress
Wintercress
Red and black spruce-pitch *

☞ * Know your evergreens. The American yew is a poisonous evergreen which is a low, straggling shrub. Needles are green on both sides.

Recipes and suggestions in this section include dried foods, as well as fresh. Refer to the Autumn Foraging section for other cold weather recipes.

UNCULTIVATED GARDEN

GENERAL SUGGESTIONS

- Needles from pine and hemlock evergreen trees can be steeped for 10 minutes to make an aromatic tea or delicious stock for cooking rice, soup, or stew. Use one small bough per quart of water; avoid boiling or you will get turpentine.
- Chives hold their heads tall and proud all winter. Even in deep snow these plants are waiting to be collected. Gather a small cluster (10-15 tops), mince, and add to soup, stew, grain, saute, or other recipes.
- Wintercress stays out all winter. Its flavor is strong and its effect invigorating. Add small amounts to stew, soup, casseroles, stir-fry, and similar preparations. Cook in several waters first to reduce the strong flavor.
- Watercress grows in springs that will flow all winter. It can become a winter forager's best friend because the mighty provider is relatively easy to collect. In spring its foliage has a burst of growth, so watercress is a substantial March-May green. Use it raw in salad or on sandwiches, or add it at the end of cooking time to water sautes, soups, or stews. The plant is comprised mostly of water; if it is cooked more than a few minutes, little will remain.
- Chickweed, garlic mustard, dandelion, plantain, and various other hardy greens will grow in certain climates all winter. Use with winter or autumn recipes.

DRIED GREENS STOCK

Steep 2-3 tablespoon dried nettle, violet leaves, lamb's quarter, amaranth, plantain or other mild-tasting, dried green in 4 cups water. Simmer for 5 minutes, but avoid boiling. Remove from flame and steep 15 minutes. Strain, if appropriate. Use as stock for soup, stew, gravy, sauce, or combine half and half with tea or organic coffee.

BARLEY PORRIDGE

Using the dried greens stock, a thick grain soup can be made with dried or fresh ingredients, depending on availability. The following is one idea, but I'm sure you can come up with other concoctions by adapting recipes or inventing new ones.

6" strip kombu seaweed, chopped (optional)
1 c. cooked barley or barley flakes
6 c. greens stock
1/4 c. dried lentils, rinsed
1 onion, peeled and diced

1/2 c. fresh wild roots, or 2 T. dried (less if harsh tasting)
6-10 mushrooms, sliced
sea salt, tamari or miso to flavor
1/2 c. fresh chickweed, if available
chives for garnish, if available

Soak the roots 30 minutes if they are dried. In a soup pot, add the grain, kombu, lentils, vegetables, and stock water. Bring to a boil, add 1/4 teaspoon sea salt, then lower heat and simmer until the vegetables are tender. Add chickweed and check the flavor. If too strong tasting, add 2 teaspoon pureed miso to mellow and provide a rich broth. Otherwise, season to preference. Garnish and serve.

WINTERCRESS AND TAHINI

Some people find wintercress too bitter to enjoy. Use of tahini and tamari subdues the harshness. If other leafy greens, such as dandelion or garlic mustard are collectible, try them instead of cress.

1 med. onion
2 c. wintercress
1 T. sesame tahini

1 t. tamari or soy sauce
few drops sesame or other oil

Spread oil on the bottom of a heavy skillet or wok. Heat, add the onions and a pinch of sea salt and saute until transparent. Stir in the greens and cook until wilted. In a separate bowl, cream the tahini with the tamari and 1/4 cup water. Add this to the greens. Cover and simmer on low heat for 10 minutes, stirring to avoid sticking.

STUFFED CABBAGE ROLLS

Cook the cabbage leaves in boiling water with a pinch of salt until they are slightly tender. Cool, then shave the hard rib at the bottom so it is thin and will easily roll. Mash the tofu and add the rest of the ingredients. Place several tablespoons of stuffing on the bottom part of the cabbage leaf. Roll tightly and secure with a toothpick if necessary. Place in a baking dish and bake at 350°, covered, for 45 minutes, then uncovered for 15 minutes. During the last 5 minutes of baking, sprinkle chives on top.

6-8 large cabbage leaves
1 lb. tofu
3 T. white miso *

1 c. watercress, finely chopped
1/2 c. onion (wild or domestic), diced
1 T. chives, finely chopped

* If miso is unavailable, use 2 teaspoons of sesame tahini, and add tamari or salt to taste.

VARIATIONS:
- Instead of watercress, try various roots or tubers. Burdock or Jerusalem artichoke are especially tasty.
- For a delicious topping, use Mock Tomato Sauce (see recipe), and bake.

WATERCRESS SUSHI

Sushi is a long-time Japanese staple. Modern preparations call for the use of white rice. I usually use brown rice, cooked with a little extra water to make it softer. In the following style of sushi, vegetables are rolled in the center. This recipe makes one roll, multiply ingredients for more.

1 sheet sushi nori seaweed
3/4 c. cooked rice
1 t. (or to taste) dijon style mustard

1/4 c. watercress, finely chopped
1 t. walnuts, minced

Place nori on a rice mat (if available) to aid rolling. Spread rice evenly on top of the sheet, leaving 1 inch along the top end and 1/2 inch at the bottom. Spread a line of mustard lengthwise about 1 inch from the bottom. Sprinkle watercress and nuts over the mustard. Beginning at the bottom, carefully roll the sushi, being sure to keep it snug. Use the mat to help roll. Wet the top edge slightly to seal the roll. Slice into 6 pieces using a wet knife.

ROOTS AND TUBERS

Hidden beneath the soil is the real storehouse of winter food. Many roots can be dug if the ground is not frozen or if you planned ahead in autumn and mulched with a layer of leaves, straw, or other organic material. In southern temperate climates, collecting and digging is fairly reliable all winter. See the Autumn Foraging introduction and root section for more information on edible roots.

COMMON WINTER ROOTS AND TUBERS

American lotus - water tuber
Arrowhead - water tuber
Burdock - root
Cattail - water root
Chicory - root
Day lily - tuber
Evening primrose - root
Ginger - rhizome
Great bulrush* - water tuber

Jerusalem artichoke - tuber
Marshmallow - root
Salsify - root
Silverweed - root
Wild carrot - root
Wild onion - bulb
Wild parsnip - root
Yellow pond lily - water tuber

 * Great bulrush - root hairs and outer rind can be scraped off.

SOFT MILLET WITH WILD PARSNIP

Millet generates a lot of internal heat. When it is pressure-cooked with wild parsnip, the results are powerful. This makes a sweet-tasting dish which is enjoyable at breakfast or anytime. Top with toasted seeds, nuts, dried fruit, milk or soy milk, or enjoy plain.

1 c. millet, washed *1 c. wild parsnip root, chopped*
4 c. boiling water *1/4 t. sea salt*

Rinse millet and place parsnips and the grain in a pressure cooker. Add boiling water and pressure-cook, with salt, for 20 minutes. Remove from heat. Let pressure come down. Mix from top to bottom. Top with toasted sesame seeds.

VARIATIONS:
- If a pressure-cooker is unavailable, simmer, covered, for 30-40 minutes.
- Use other wild roots or tubers: wild carrot, day lily tubers, marsh mallow, thistle, or wild onion.
- Try the same dish with whole oats or soft wheat berries and pressure-cook for 65 minutes. Soak grain overnight before cooking.

SWEET RICE, BURDOCK ROOT, AND SQUASH

This is one of my favorite flavor combinations. Make enough for lunch left-overs because the texture and taste is even better the next day.

2 c. sweet rice (or brown rice) *3 1/2 c. water*
1/3 c. burdock root, chopped thin *pinch sea salt*
1 c. sweet winter squash

Rinse the grain. Place the rice and vegetables in the pressure cooker with the rice on the bottom, the squash next, and the burdock on top. Add water. Bring to a low boil and add a pinch of sea salt. Cover and bring to pressure, then reduce the flame and allow to cook at low pressure for 45 minutes. Use a flame tamer to avoid scorching. Allow the pressure to come down slowly. Serve warm.

VARIATION:
- If a pressure-cooker is unavailable, simmer on low heat for 1 hour using 6 cups water (instead of 3-1/2 cups).

BUCKWHEAT PATTIES

Buckwheat is a traditional grain of Northern Europe and Russia where its heat-producing qualities have kept people warm for centuries. Used in this recipe, patties are baked and topped with spicy mustard. These look a lot like the all-American favorite, hamburgers. I have taken them to a barbecue party

4 c. stock (see stock recipe above)
2 c. buckwheat groats, washed
1 c. onion, diced
1 c. mild tasting wild root or tuber, grated
(if dried, 1/4 c. soaked 30 min.) *
1 c. celery, diced

1 t. cumin
pinch sea salt
1 t. tamari
flour
spicy mustard

and put them on the grill for a few minutes to absorb some charcoal flavor. Worked great. New vegetarians often appreciate a hint of the old days.

Bring stock to a boil. Meanwhile, place the buckwheat in a hot skillet and dry-roast 4-5 minutes, stirring constantly. Add groats to the boiling liquid, then add onions, roots and salt. Cover and bring to a boil. Reduce the flame and simmer on low heat for 20 minutes without stirring. Stir in celery, cumin and tamari and cook 2-3 minutes more. Place in a bowl and allow to cool. Add 1/2 cup flour (rice or whole wheat flour works well), stir and form into patties which are firm and hamburger-sized. Add more flour if necessary to mold. Place on a greased cookie sheet and bake at 350° for approximately 40 minutes, or until golden brown on top and cooked throughout. Top with spicy mustard and bake 5 minutes longer. Serve plain or on a bun with lettuce.

* Jerusalem artichoke, wild parsnip, marsh mallow, wild carrot, dandelion, thistle, or one half the amount of wild onion bulbs. Burdock would taste OK, but it is really to yang, I feel, to add to buckwheat.

BURDOCK-CARROT KINPIRA

Kinpira is a traditional Japanese style of preparing root vegetables to increase their ki. The recipe strengthens intestines and is especially good for men. Note that numerous variations are possible by using other root vegetables, domestic and/or wild.

1 part fresh burdock root, shaved in thin pieces
2-3 parts domestic carrot, shaved thicker and wider

1 t. sesame oil
pinch of sea salt
dash tamari (soy sauce) to taste

Heat oil in a heavy skillet or wok. Add carrots and burdock, then saute 5 minutes over medium flame. Add a pinch of sea salt and enough water to cover the bottom of the skillet. Cover and simmer until tender. Add tamari, then stir and simmer 1-2 minutes longer. If desired, sprinkle toasted sesame seeds or chopped fresh chives over the top before serving.

VARIATIONS:
- Use other wild roots or tubers such as Jerusalem artichoke, parsnip, or salsify.
- Use other domestic roots such as parsnip, rutabaga, turnip, or daikon radish.

BUCKWHEAT RAMEN WITH ROOTS

Ramen noodle porridge offers a fast, working person's lunch. Children usually enjoy it too. Select whole grain ramen noodles (or use other whole grain pasta) from a reliable health food store or co-op. I often use buckwheat noodles in winter to create extra internal heat. Dried greens and roots work well in this dish. Soak dried roots for 30 minutes first to reconstitute them. Use the soaking water for stock.

1 pkg. buckwheat ramen noodles (or other)
*1-2 c. available vegetables, chopped ***
*1/4-1/2 c. wild root or tuber ***
4 c. stock made from simmering

1 T. dried greens
1 T. chopped chives, watercress or 1/4 c. dried dulse
seasoning to taste

In a saucepan, bring the liquid to a boil. Add vegetables, then noodles. Simmer over low heat for 7-10 minutes until noodles are soft. Season with 1 teaspoon miso or other seasoning. Serve topped with minced chives, watercress, or dried dulse added at the end. For thicker consistency, use 3 cups of liquid.

* Usable vegetables include: onion, rutabaga, turnip, carrot, parsnip, cauliflower, cabbage, celery, et cetera.
* Usable wild root vegetables include: burdock, wild parsnip, salsify, silverweed, Jerusalem artichoke, evening primrose, day lily, or arrowhead.

COFFEE SUBSTITUTE

The following combination offers a nourishing caffeine-free substitute for coffee and is similar in flavor. If roasted chicory or dandelion root were used alone, it would be a very bitter drink for some. Adjust the amount of root to taste. Bitter flavor is often lacking in our diets, but it is important to include foods which have this quality. They stimulate the heart and improve circulation. The recipe makes enough for numerous servings.

4 cups whole barley berries (hulled or unhulled), rinsed

10-20 dandelion or chicory roots, scrubbed clean

Preheat oven to 350°. Drain the rinsed barley and spread it evenly and thinly over 2 cookie sheets. On a separate cookie tray, spread the roots, chopped to a consistent size. Bake until they are toasted brown and the roots are dry. Hulled barley takes longer to roast (several hours sometimes). The root may be ready in less that 30 minutes. Store the two separately in air-tight glass jars. (Collect roots in early winter before the ground freezes.)

For a smaller quantity, try the following barley coffee:

> 1/4 c. roasted barley
> 1 t. roasted dandelion or chicory root
> 4 c. water

Bring to a simmer and cook 15-30 minutes until water is dark and rich-tasting. Further simmering gives the drink a creamy consistency.

MOCHA PUDDING

Once the above drink is made, a yummy dessert can be prepared quite simply.

2 c. roasted barley and dandelion (or chicory) root tea
2-3 heaping T. barley malt syrup

1 T. tahini
2 T. kudzu root
1/4 c. water

Prepare the drink as indicated in the recipe above. In a saucepan, mix barley malt and tahini until well-creamed. Add a small amount of barley coffee and cream this into the first mixture. Keep adding small amounts until all has been added. Bring to a gentle boil. Dissolve kudzu in 1/4 cup of cool water and stir this slowly into the mocha mixture. Cook until thick, stirring constantly. Let cool and serve as pudding or pie filling, or use as a frosting for a couscous cake. Top with chopped nuts, if desired.

VARIATIONS:
- Soak dried fruit for 30 minutes, chop and add with kudzu, or add fresh fruit.
- Other thickeners can be used in place of kudzu.

GINGER FISH

Spread oil into a heavy frying pan, heat and add ginger. Saute 2-3 minutes. Baste fillets with tamari, and add to the hot skillet. Reduce heat to low and slow-cook until tender. Turn the fillets with a spatula when cooked on the first side. Garnish with minced chives.

1/2" wild ginger tuber, minced (collected before frost)
1 t. toasted sesame oil (or 1 T. other)

1 lb. fish fillets (perch, cod, haddock, bass, flounder, etc.)
1/2 t. tamari

FRUITS AND BERRIES

The fruits of winter are tiny, compact, and generally reddish in color. Many yang characteristics manifest to create fruit which is very strengthening compared to the lush, expansive fruits of summer and early autumn. Winter fruit often contains significant amounts of vitamins A, B_2 (riboflavin), and C. Remember this food is an important staple for wildlife, so pick with awareness of their needs.

COMMON WINTER FRUITS AND BERRIES

American hackberry
Bayberry
Black crowberry - north
Cranberry *
Ground cherry

Juniper berries
Persimmon - early winter
Rose hips
Wintergreen berries

☞ * The cranberry has three species: large bush, small bush, and mountain. All grow in northern regions and all are edible, although each is quite different.

ADDITIONAL SUGGESTIONS

- Ground cherries and cranberries can be found in the snow. Usually by mid-winter both are gone.
- Rose hips may stay on sprawling vines all winter. Look for them in meadows. (According to Euell Gibbons, one rose hip contains as much vitamin C as 10 to 12 **dozen** oranges.) Steep 6-12 hips in 4 cups of water for tea. Strain.
- Persimmons often linger into early winter. (See the Autumn Foraging section for several persimmon recipes.)
- Juniper berries, wintergreen, and bayberry are pleasant as seasoning, especially in fish soup.

UNCULTIVATED GARDEN

CRANBERRY SAUCE

Our family enjoys this recipe for winter holiday meals or as a marmalade substitute on bread. Try it as a topping for buckwheat pancakes too. Wild cranberries are tiny and sometimes difficult to find. They grow mostly in northern wetlands and fragile habitats. You might add a few wild cranberries to those you buy.

2 c. cranberries, washed & cleaned
1/2 c. raisins
1/4 c. barley malt

3-4 T. kudzu
1 1/2 c. water or apple juice

Cook the raisins in 1 cup water for about 10 minutes. Add cranberries, the remaining water, a pinch of sea salt, and the barley malt. Bring to a boil, reduce the flame to low and simmer about 10 minutes. Dilute kudzu in a little cool water and add to the cranberries, stirring constantly to avoid lumping or burning. Simmer another 5 minutes. Pour into a mold or bowl and allow to thicken.

ROSE HIP SYRUP

Rose hips have a mild, sour flavor which can be very appetizing as a syrup or spread for hot muffins.

2 c. apple juice or water
1 stick cinnamon, or spicebush
3 handfuls rose hips
pinch sea salt

2-4 T. maple syrup, barley malt, or half each
2 T. kudzu, or arrowroot powder

Bring the liquid and cinnamon almost to a boil, then simmer 5 minutes. Remove from heat, add salt and rose hips, then steep for 45 minutes. Strain liquid into a pan and add sweetener. In a cup, add a little cool water to kudzu and stir to dissolve. Add this to the liquid and simmer, stirring constantly until thickened. Next, remove the cinnamon stick from the fruit and mash the pulp through a food mill or strainer to remove the seeds. Add pulp to the liquid and mix. (Take the seeds out for birds to enjoy.) Use as is for syrup. Save some to add to dried fruit and cook this for a compote or fruit shortcake.

HOLIDAY PUNCH

Simmer the above down to 1/3 of its original volume. Mash to a pulp, strain, and add this liquid to 2 quarts of your favorite sparkling water. Top with thin orange slices or other fruit.

1/2 c. rose hips
1 1/2 qt. fruit juice (apple, cherry, strawberry, raspberry)
15 juniper berries
20 hemlock needles
2 qt. sparkling water

CONCLUSION

For years, I would walk to a cluster of edible plants, give them an offering of prayer, and state my intentions to collect. "Who wants to become human?" I would announce, as though this were a big honor. After all, we humans are the highest and most evolved species.

One winter morning, after eating a small breakfast of wild greens, I walked to a cluster of watercress and stated my offer to evolve it to human status. Immediately, I was struck with the supreme arrogance of my statement. In an instant, I was humbled to realize the insignificance of my life compared to that of a plant.

Plants provide food, medicine, shelter, and clothing. They give off oxygen for the continuation of all life. They filter pollutants from the air. They stop soil erosion. They help the soil become loose and porous so it can absorb water. Through transpiration, they evaporate water back into the air to help form rain clouds. Weeds grow in particular areas in order to release their nutrients and enrich the soil. The remains of dead plants make possible the fossil fuels which transport us, and keep us warm at night.

On the basic cellular level, plants transform light to energy by photosynthesis. Once light is contained in chemical form, it can be transformed as an energy source for all other organisms, including humans.

"What do I do compared to all this?" I pondered. Mostly, I take. The realization came that I was the one being honored by incorporating the plant into my being.

Triggered by this insight, I remembered a sermon I once heard in which the pastor stated that "dominion over" had possibly been mistranslated. Another meaning could be "protector of." On that sunny January morning, it became obvious to me that our human role is not to arrogantly dominate and alter the natural order, but to facilitate it much as a conductor directs musicians, allowing each to play to his or her fullest potential.

If we humbly help the rhythms and harmonies of nature to flow with the way of ki, then we can truly be at peace.

ENDNOTES

1. *Mother Earth News,* November/December, 1979. Rodale Press. Emmaus, PA and *Stalking the Healthful Herbs,* by Euell Gibbons, David McKay Co.Inc., New York, 1970.

2. From an article written by Gar Hildenbrand, entitled "A Question of Life and Death", which appeared in issue NL 24 and 25, 1988, of *The Healing Newsletter*, published by the Gerson Institute, P.O. Box 430, Bonita, CA 92002.

3. *The News Bulletin* of the National Coalition Against the Misuse of Pesticides (NCAMP), 530 7th St., S.E., Washington, DC 20003. October, 1988 issue of NCAMP'S Technical Report.

4. Refer to *Biological Transmutations,* by Louis Kervran, Swan House, 1972. For further information on biological transmutations, consult *Guardians of the Soil,* by Joseph Concanover, Devin-Adair Co., 1950, and *An Acres U.S.A. Primer*, by Charles Walters, Jr., and C. J. Fenzau; Access U.S.A., 1979.

5. Natural Agriculture is a modern term for a system which advocates growing a variety of crops together in one field, along with careful management of weeds. The soil is neither plowed nor cultivated. Non-hybrid plants reseed themselves year after year and weeds are mowed or mulched. This kind of system seems strange and chaotic to those accustomed to straight rows with one crop and no weeds. However, yields from Natural Agriculture fields are found to be comparable to yields from monoculture systems. The ki of food grown in the former is far higher. The time and expense involved in growing the crops is also much less. Natural Agriculture supports small scale, family farms. For more information on Natural Agriculture, read *One Straw Revolution,* by Masanobu Fukuoka, Rodale Press, Emmaus, PA, 1978, and his more in-depth book *The Natural Way of Farming (Theory and Practice of Green Philosophy),* Japan Publications, New York, 1985.

6. For in-depth discussions of weeds and soil use, see *Acres USA Primer,* by Charles Walter, and C. J. Fenzau, Acres USA, 1979; *Weeds, Guardian of the Soil,* by Joseph A. Cocannouer, The Devin-Adair Co. 1976; and *Weeds and What They Tell,* by Ehrenfriede Pfeiffer, Rodale Press, 1976.

7. *PARACELSUS - His Mystical and Medical Philosphy,* 1964, by Manly P. Hall, The Philosophical Research Society, Inc., 3910 Los Feliz Boulevard, Los Angeles, California 90027.

8. For further information on the subject, refer to *The Wisdom of the Body,* Walter Cannon, W.W. Norton Co.,1932 and *Food and Healing,* Annemarie Colbin, Ballantine Books, 1986.

9. For more information and numerous essences, contact the Flower Essence Society, P.O. Box 459, Nevada City, CA 95959.

10. Several reliable seaweed sources are : Maine Coast Sea Vegetables, Shore Rd., Franklin, ME 04634, 207-565-2907; Maine Seaweed Co., P.O. Box 57, Wilderness Shore Rd., Steuben, ME 04680, 207-546-2875; Maritime Foods, 43 Chase St., South Portland, ME 04106, 207-767-5968.

GLOSSARY

AGAR-AGAR - A clear gelatin which is processed from a sea vegetable, dried, and made into bars, flakes, or powder, and used in kanten or aspics.

ARAME - A sea vegetable which is commercially available dried. It is black in color and extremely high in nutrients. Reconstituted, arame is used along with other vegetables, cooked, or raw in salad.

ARROWROOT - The root of a common water plant, used as a thickening agent for sauces, stews, casseroles, or fruit desserts; also used for tempura batter.

BANCHA TEA - The twigs and stems from the Japanese tea bush, low in caffine, also known as **KUKICHA** in Japanese.

BARLEY MALT - A grain sweetener made from concentrated amounts of roasted whole barley.

BROWN RICE VINEGAR - Vinegar made from brown rice.

BULGUR - A product of whole wheat which is cracked, lightly boiled, and dried.

COUSCOUS - Cracked whole wheat which is partially refined.

FLAME TAMER - Metal screen or disk placed under a pressure cooker or cooking pan to prevent burning by evenly distributing the heat.

FOOD MILL - A non-electric hand mill used to puree foods.

GOMASHIO - A condiment made of toasted sesame seeds and sea salt, then ground.

HIZIKI - (Sometimes spelled hijiki) A sea vegetable which contains a high level of calcium. Available commercially, dried. Reconstituted, it is cooked with vegetables.

INTERNATIONAL UNITS (I.U.) - A unit of measurement for amounts of vitamins and minerals in food.

KANTEN - A gelled dessert made from agar-agar seaweed.

KI - Life force.

KINPIRA - A Japanese-style of sauteing root vegetables in a small amount of water and tamari

KOMBU - A robust sea vegetable which is harvested and dried for commercial sale. Very high in nutrients, it is used to enrich soup stock, stew, grains, beans, and vegetables.

KUKICHA - See bancha tea.

KUZU - Also known as **KUDZU**. Obtained from the root of a prolific southern vine. Use as a thickener for gravies, sauces, soups, desserts, and certain medicinal drinks.

MIRIN - A cooking wine made from sweet rice.

MISO - A fermented and aged paste which is made from soybeans, sea salt, and grain (usually rice or barley). Used to enrich soup, stew, spreads, and sauces with a salty/sweet flavor.

NORI - A sea vegetable which is commercially processed into thin sheets. Black or purlple in color, the sheets turn dark green when lightly toasted over a flame. They are used in traditional Japanese cooking for sushi rolls and rice balls. It is also cut in thin strips and used for soup garnish or cooked with tamari for a condiment.

PRESSURE COOK - To cook in an air-tight metal pressure cooker.

PUREE - To mash food in a bowl, mill, Japanese suribachi, or food processor until of even consistency.

RAMEN - A Chinese-sytle noodle that has been deep-fried and dried for quick cooking. Used plain or in soups.

RICE SYRUP - A natural sweetener made from malted brown rice.

SAUTE - To lightly fry in a skillet or wok.

SEA SALT - Salt which is obtained from the ocean. Unlike refined salt, it is high in trace minerals and contains no chemicals or sugar.

STEAM - Cook on a rack over boiling water.

STIR-FRY - Similar to saute, using small amount of oil, high heat, and continuous stirring.

SUKIYAKI - Traditional Japanese one-dish meal. Cooked in a deep skillet, using a variety of vegetables, noodles, tofu, or other ingredients.

TAHINI - A thick nut butter made from ground sesame seeds.

TAMARI - Traditionally, a soy sauce which is unrefined. Also known as shoyu, it is a by-product of miso-making. Used as a salty flavoring for cooking or condiment.

TEMPURA - To deep-fry until golden-brown sliced vegetables or other items which have been dipped in batter. Usually served with a salty or pungent dipping sauce.

TOFU - Soybean curd made from cooking soybeans. High in protein, it can be purchased commercially in small cakes and is used for cooking with vegetables or pureed for sauces and dressings.

UDON NOODLES - A style of Japanese whole-grain noodle which is flat with sguared edges.

UMEBOSHI VINEGAR - Called ume-su in Japanese, it is vinegar made from pickled (umeboshi) plums.

REFERENCES

WILD FOOD IDENTIFICATION AND BACKGROUND

Angier Bradford, *Feasting Free on Wild Edibles,* Pyramid Communications, New York, 1975.

Angier, Bradford, *Field Guide to Edible Wild Plants,* Stackpole Books, Harrisburg, Pennsylvania, 1974.

Brown, Tom Jr., *Tom Brown's Guide to Wild Edible and Medicinal Plants,* Berkley Books, New York, 1985.

Cocannover, Joseph A. *Weeds-Guardians of the Soil,* The Devin-Adair Co., Old Grennwich, Connecticut.

Densmore, Frances, *How Indians Use Wild Plants for Food, Medicine, and Crafts,* Dover Publications, New York, 1974.

Devignes, Antoine, *How to Recognize 30 Edible Mushrooms,* Barron's Educational Series, Inc., Woodbury, New York, 1976.

Elliot, Douglas B., *Roots, An Underground Botany and Forager's Guide*, The Chatham Press, Old Greenwich, Connecticut, 1976.

Fernald, Merritt Lyndon and Kinsey, Alfred Charles, *Wild Edible Plants of Eastern North America,* Idlewild Press, Cornwall-on-Hudson, New York, 1943.

Gibbons, Euell, *Stalking the Blue-Eyed Scallop,* David McKay Company, New York, 1973.

Gibbons, Euell, *Stalking the Healthful Herbs,* David McKay Company, New York, 1970.

Gibbons, Euell, *Stalking the Wild Asparagus,* David McKay Company, New York, 1972.

Hall, Alan, *The Wild Food Trail Guide*, Holt, Rinehart & Winston, New York, 1976.

Hardin, James W. and Arena, Jay M. M.D., *Human Poisoning From Native and Cultivated Plants*, Duke University Press, 1974.

Harris, Ben Charles, *Eat the Weeds*, Barre Publishers, Barre, Massachusetts, 1972.

Kavasch, Barrie, *Native Harvests*, Vintage Books, New York, 1979.

Kindscher, Kelly, *Wild Edible Plants of the Prairie*, University Press of Kansas, Lawrence, Kansas, 1987.

Kingsbury, John M., *Poisonous Plants of the United States*, Prentiss Hall, 1964.

Kirk, Donald, R., *Wild Edible Plants of the Western United States*, Naturegraph Publications, Healdsburg, California, 1970.

Martin, Alexander C., Zim, Herbert S., and Nelson, Arnold L., *American Wildlife & Plants - A Guide to Wildlife Food Habits*, Dover Publications, NYC, 1951.

Medsger, Oliver Perry, *Edible Wild Plants*, Collier Books, New York, 1966.

Miller, Dorcas S., *Berry Finder*, Nature Study Guide, Berkeley, California, 1986.

Peterson, Lee Allen, *Edible Wild Plants*, Peterson Field Guides, Houghton Mifflin Company, Boston, 1977.

Pfeiffer, Ehrenfried E., *Weeds and What They Tell*, Bio-Dynamic Farming and Gardening Association, Inc., Springfield, Illinois, 1976.

Phillips, Jan, *Wild Edibles of Missouri*, Missouri Department of Conservation, 1979.

Phillips, Roger, *Wild Foods*, Pan Books Ltd, London, 1983.

Russell, Helen Ross, *Foraging for Dinner*, Thomas Nelson Publishers, Nashville, 1975.

Saunders, Charles Francis, *Edible and Useful Wild Plants of the U.S. and Canada*, Dover Publications, New York, 1976.

Scully, Virginia, *A Treasury of American Indian Herbs,* Bonanza Books, New York, 1970.

Tatum, Billy Joe, *Billy Joe Tatum's Wild Foods Field Guide and Cookbook*, Workman Publishing Company, New York, 1976.

Tompkins, Peter and Bird, Christopher, *The Secret Life of Plants,* Avon Books, New York, 1974.

How to Survive on Land and Sea, United States Naval Institute, Annapolis, Maryland, 1943.

Northern Survival, Charles Scribner's Sons, New York, 1979.

Watts, Mary Theilgaard, *Flower Finder,* Nature Study Guide, Berkeley, California, 1955.

Watts, Mary Thielgaard, *Master Tree Finder,* Nature Study Guide, Berkeley, California, 1963.

HERBS AND HERBAL MEDICINE

Angier, Bradford, *Field Guide to Medicinal Wild Plants,* Stackpole Books, Harrisburg, Pennsylvania, 1978.

Chancellor, Dr. Philip M., *Bach Flower Remedies,* Keats Publishing, Inc., New Canaan, Connecticut, 1971.

Geuter, Maria, *Herbs in Nutrition,* Bio-Dynamic Agriculture Assoc., London. 1978.

Grieve, Mrs. M., *A Modern Herbal,* Dover Publications, Inc., New York, 1971.

Hylton, William H., *The Rodale Herb Book,* Rodale Press Book Division, Emmaus, Pennsylvania, 1979.

Hoffman, David, *The Holistic Herbal,* Findhorn Press, Forres, Scotland. 1986.

Kloss, Jethro, *Back to Eden,* Lifetime Books, Riverside, California, 1973.

Lust, John, *The Herb Book,* Bantam Books, New York, 1980.

Tierra, Michael, *The Way of Herbs,* Washington Square Press, New York, 1983.

Weiner, Michael A., *Earth Medicines - Earth Foods,* Collier Books, New York, 1972.

MACROBIOTICS AND NATURAL AGRICULTURE

Aihara, Herman, *Basic Macrobiotics,* Japan Publications, Inc., Tokyo and New York, 1985.

Aihara, Herman, *Natural Healing Through Macrobiotics,* Japan Publications, Inc., Tokyo and New York, 1983.

Colbin, Annemarie, *Food and Healing,* Ballantine Books, New York, 1986.

Esko, Edward and Wendy, *Macrobiotic Cooking for Everyone,* Japan Publication's Inc., Tokyo and New York.

Fukuoka, Masanobu, *The One-Straw Revolution, An Introduction To Natural Farming,* Rodale Press, Emmaus, Pennsylvania.

Fukuoku, Masanobu, *The Natural Way of Farming,* Japan Publications, Inc. Tokyo and New York, 1985.

Haas, Elson, M.D. *Staying Healthy With The Seasons,* Celestial Arts, Berkeley, California, 1981.

Jackson, Wes, Berry, Wendall and Colman, Bruce, *Meeting the Expectations of the Land,* North Point Press, San Francisco, 1984.

Kushi, Aveline and Jack, Alex, *Complete Guide to Macrobiotic Healing,* Warner Communications Co., New York, 1985,

Kushi, Michio and Jack, Alex, *The Book of Macrobiotics,* Japan Publications, Inc., Tokyo and New York. 1987.

Kushi, Michio, *Natural Healing Through Macrobiotics,* Japan Publications, Inc., Tokyo and New York.

Ohsawa, George, *The Book of Judgement,* Ohsawa Foundation, Los Angeles, California.

Ohsawa, George, *The Unique Principle,* George Ohsawa Foundation Macrobiotic Foundation, Oroville, California.

Ohsawa, George, *Zen Macrobiotics,* Ohsawa Foundation, Los Angles, California.

Veith, Ilza, *The Yellow Emperior's Classic of Internal Medicine,* University of California Press, Berkeley, California.

Muramoto, Naboru, *Healing Ourselves,* Avon Books, New York, 1973.

Schumacher, E.F., *Small Is Beautiful,* Harper and Row, New York, 1975.

Walters, Charles Jr. and Fenzau, C.J., *An Acres U.S.A. Primer,* Acres U.S.A., Raytown, Missouri, 1979.

Weed, Susun, *Healing Wise,* Ashtree Publishing Co., Woodstock, New York, 1989.

RELATED READING

Bockemuhl, Jochen, *In Partnership With Nature,* Bio-Dynamic Literature, Wyoming, Rhode Island, 1981.

Fischman, Dr. Walter and Grimms, Dr. Mark, *Muscle Response Test,* Richard Marek Publishers, New York, 1979.

Martin, Alexander C., Zim, Herbert S., and Nelson, Arnold L., *American Wildlife & Plants - A Guide to Wildlife Food Habits,* Dover Publications, 1951.

Thie, John F. and Marks, Mary, *Touch For Health,* DeVorss and Co. Santa Monica, California, 1973.

Shepard, Dr. Stephen Paul, *Healing Energies,* Biworld Publisher, Provo, Utah, 1983.

Steiner, Rudolf, *Agriculture,* Bio-Dynamic Agricultural Assoc., London, 1974.

Steiner, Rudolf, *Cosmic Memory,* Harper and Row, New York. 1981.

Wright, Machaelle Small, *Behaving As If The God In All Things Mattered,* Parelandra, Ltd., Jeffersonton, Virginia, 1987.

Wright, Machaelle Small, *The Perelandra Garden Workbook,* Perelandra, Ltd., Jeffersonton, Virginia, 1988.

COMMON NAMES AND GENERA

ACORN - Quercus
ALFALFA - Medicago
AMARANTH - Amaranthus
AMERICAN HACKBERRY - Celtis
AMERICAN LOTUS - Nelumbo
APPLES - Pyrus
ARROWHEAD - Sagittaria
BARBERRY - Berberis
BASIL - Ocimum
BAYBERRY - Myrica
BEECH - Fagus
BERGAMOT - Monarda
BIRCH - Monarda
BLACKBERRY - Rubus
BLACK CHERRY - Prunus
BLACK CROWBERRY - Empetrum
BLACK LOCUST - Robinia
BLACK WALNUT - Juglans
BLUEBERRY - Vaccinium, Gaylussacia
BRACKEN FERN - Pteridium
BURDOCK - Arctium
BUTTERNUT - Juglans
CAMOMILE - Anthemis
CARAWAY - Carum
CATBRIER - Smilex
CATNIP - Nepeta
CATTAIL - Typha
CHESTNUT - Castanea
CHICKWEED - Stellaria, Alsine
CHICORY - Chichorium
CHINQUAPIN - Castanea
CHIVES - Allium
CHOKECHERRY - Prunus
CHUFA - Cyperus
CLEAVERS - Galium
CLOVER - Trifolium
COLTSFOOT - Tussilago
COMFREY - Symphytum
CRABAPPLE - Pyrus
CRANBERRY - Vaccinium, Viburnum
CURRANTS - Ribes
DANDELION - Taraxacum
DAY LILY - Hemerocallis
DEWBERRY - Rubus
DOCK - Rumex
DULSE - Rhodymenia
EASTERN HEMLOCK - Tsuga
ELDERBERRY - Sambucus
EVENING PRIMROSE - Oenothera
GILL-OVER-THE-GROUND - Glechoma
GLASSWORT - Salicornia
GOOSEBERRY - Ribes
GRAPE - Vitis
GREAT BULRUSH - Scirpus
GROUND CHERRY - Physalis
GROUNDNUT - Apios
HAWTHORN - Crataegus
HAZELNUT - Corylus
HICKORY - Carya
HORSERADISH - Armoracia
HORSETAIL - Equisetum
HUCKLEBERRY - Vaccinium,

JAPANESE KNOTWEED - Polygonum
JERUSALEM ARTICHOKE - Helianthus
JUNEBERRY - Amelanchier
JUNIPER - Juniperus
KELP - Nereocystis
KINNIKINIK - Arctostaphylos
LABRADOR TEA - Ledum
LAMB'S QUARTER - Chenopodium
LARGE CANE - Arundinaria
LETTUCE SAXIFRAGE - Saxifrage
MALLOWS - Malva
MAY APPLE - Podophyllum
MILKWEED - Asclepias
MILLET - Pucium
MINER'S LETTUCE - Montia
MINT - Mentha
MOUNTAIN ASH - Pyrus
MOUNTAIN SORREL - Oxyria
MUGWORT - Artemisia
MULBERRY - Morus
MULLEIN - Brassica
NETTLES - Utrica
NEW JERSEY TEA - Ceanothus
ONION - Allium
OSTRICH FERN - Pteretis
PAWPAW - Asimina
PECAN - Carya
PEPPERGRASS - Lepidium
PERSIMMON - Diospyros
PINEAPPLE WEED - Matricaria
PINES - Pinus
PINON - Pinus
PLANTAIN - Plantago
POKEWEED - Phytolacca
POND LILY - Nuphar
PRAIRIE TURNIP - Psoralea

PRICKLY PEAR - Opuntia
PURSLANE - Portulaca
RASPBERRY - Cercis
REED - Phragmites
ROSE - Rosa
SAGE - Salvia
SALSIFY - Tragopogon
SANDHILL PLUM - Prunus
SASSAFRAS - Sassafras
SHEPERD'S PURSE - Capsella
SILVERWEED - Potentilla
SORRELS - Rumex
SPICEBUSH - Benzoin
SPRUCES - Picea
STRAWBERRY - Rhus
SUNFLOWER - Nelianthus
SWEET GOLDENROD - Solidago
THISTLES - Sonchus
THYME - Thymus
TOOTHWORT - Dentaria
VIOLET - Viola
WALNUT - Juglans
WATERCRESS - Nasturtium
WILD APPLE - Malus, Pyrus
WILD CARROT - Daucus
WILD CHERRY - Prunus
WILD GINGER - Asarum
WILD LEEK - Allium
WILD LETTUCE - Lactuca
WILD ONION - Allium
WILD PARSNIP - Pastinaca
WILD PLUM - Prunus
WILD RAISIN - Viburnum
WILD RED CHERRY - Prunus
WILD RICE - Zizania
WINTERCRESS - Barbarea
WINTERGREEN - Gaultheria
WOOD SORREL - Oxalis
YARROW - Achillea

INDEX

Acorn, 147-148, 151
Agar-agar, 104
Alaria, 158
Alcohol, 49
Alfalfa, 112
Amaranth, 91, 94-95, 109, 122-125, 143, 145, 159
Antihydrotic, 114
Antiseptic, 114
Antispasmodic, 114
Apple, 97, 117-120, 148-153, 155
Arame, 16, 158
Aroma, 28, 35, 41-42, 45, 50-53, 69
Arrowhead, 125, 162, 166
Arrowroot, 104, 107, 119-120, 126-127, 135, 150, 154
Astringent, 114

Bach, Edward, 101
Banana, 46
Bancha, 113
Baneberry, 41
Barberry, 151
Barley, 106-107, 160, 166-167
Barley malt, 105, 146, 149-150, 152, 167, 169
Basil, 114-115
Bayberry, 168
Bean, 82, 93, 106-107, 126
Bell pepper, 95
Bergamot, 41, 96, 112, 114-115, 117
Berries, 41, 46, 62, 83-84, 99, 101, 103-104, 109-110, 112, 115, 117-121, 136, 144, 148-153, 155, 163, 168-169
Black locust, 102
Blackberry, 41, 46, 112, 118, 120
Bladder, 62, 114
Blood, 4, 6, 25-27, 60-61, 63, 89-90, 98, 101, 109, 113-114, 117, 127
Blueberry, 41, 46, 118-121, 144, 151, 153, 155
Brain, 31, 33-36
Broccoli, 125, 133, 142
Brussel sprout, 125, 133, 145
Buckwheat, 100, 164-165, 169
Bulgur, 142
Bulrush, 133, 143, 162
Burdock, 7, 26-27, 37, 47, 49-51, 84, 88, 99, 125-126, 130, 133-136, 142, 144, 157, 161-166

Cabbage, 117, 123-125, 133, 140, 142, 161, 166
Cactus, 46
Caffeine, 113
Calcium, 16, 26, 157
Camomile, 112-113
Cane, 143
Caraway, 114, 117
Carrot (wild and domestic), 18, 36-37, 39, 96, 99-100, 116, 122, 124-127, 133-135, 138-139, 142, 145, 162-166
Catbrier, 91-92
Catnip, 91, 112-113
Cattail, 27, 37, 42, 91-92, 96, 99, 107, 162

Cauliflower, 125, 133
Cautions, 9-10, 84
Cayce, Edgar, 67
Celery, 142, 145, 164, 166
Centrifugal force, 31-33
Centripetal force, 31-32
Cheese, 50, 82, 88
Cherry, 118-120, 151, 155
Chestnut, 147-149
Chi, See also: Ki, 16
Chickweed, 37, 91, 94, 100, 122, 125, 159-160
Chicory, 91, 94, 126, 134-135, 157, 162, 166
Chives, 25, 90-91, 94, 134, 141, 148, 157-159, 161, 165-167
Chokecherry, 118, 151, 153, 155
Chufa, 126, 143
Circulatory system, 109
Cleavers, 91, 100
Clover (red and white), 92, 102, 112
Coffee, 49, 113, 159, 166
Collards, 124
Color, 28, 35, 38-41, 51, 53, 55, 61, 69, 77
Coltsfoot, 91, 112, 114
Comfrey, 91, 94, 109, 112, 114, 122, 125
Corn, 62
Cornstarch, 107
Couscous, 121
Crabapple, 118, 151, 155
Cranberry, 46, 148-151, 155, 168-169
Crowberry, 151
Currant, 118, 137, 150-151, 155

Daikon, 125, 165
Dairy, 82, 106
Dandelion, 4, 6, 8, 11, 15, 26, 37, 39-41, 43-45, 64-65, 77, 87-88, 90-92, 94, 102, 109, 114, 122-123, 126, 132, 134-135, 137-142, 148, 157-160, 164, 166
Day lily, 7, 87, 92, 94, 97, 99-100, 114, 117, 125-127, 162-163, 166
Death camas, 91, 132
Dewberry, 112, 118
Dillweed, 115
Dock (curly and broad-leaf), 4, 7, 15-16, 87, 91, 94-95, 122, 125, 138, 140, 143
Doctrine of Signatures, 25, 29
Doctrine of Similars, 25
Dogbane, 40
Drugs, 32, 49, 51
Drying & dried foods, 131, 136-138, 140-142, 144-145, 147, 149-150
Dulse, 140-141, 158, 166

Earth's Force, 31, 33
Egg, 50, 82, 88, 107
Egui, 43, 55
Elder (elderberry & elderbow), 10, 102-103, 112, 114, 118-120, 151, 153
Evening primrose, 132, 134-135, 162, 166
Evergreen, 46, 157, 159

Fat, 106
Ferns, 48, 91
Fertilizer, 16, 20-21
Fish, 110, 115, 117, 127, 137

Index

Five Transformations, 5, 57-59, 61, 66, 158
Flowers, 33-35, 41-42, 46, 48, 50, 55, 65, 69, 74, 83, 88, 92, 96, 100-103, 105, 109-112, 116-117, 123
Fruit, 5, 9-10, 13, 17, 19-20, 22, 33-35, 41, 46-50, 55, 62, 82-84, 88, 101, 103-105, 109-110, 117-118, 120-121, 127, 129-130, 149-155, 163, 167-170

Gall bladder, 26, 62-64
Garlic, 25, 116
Ginger, 37, 126-127, 129, 134, 137, 162
Ginsing, 50
Glasswort, 91
Goldenrod, 112
Gooseberry, 103-104, 118-120
Grains, 17, 34, 46, 48, 61-62, 82-83, 88, 94, 98-99, 129-131, 134, 136, 138, 142-143, 145, 151, 159-160, 163-165
Grape, 41, 46, 91-92, 95-96, 118, 122, 151-152, 155
Grapefruit, 46
Greens, 4-7, 9, 11, 34, 40, 42-43, 47-48, 50, 55, 83, 87-90, 93-95, 99-100, 109-111, 116, 121-125, 157-160, 165
Grits, 142
Ground cherry, 151
Ground nut, 126-127

Habitat, 25, 27-28, 35, 44-46, 69, 73, 77
Hackberry, 151
Hawthorn, 151
Hazelnut, 144
Heart, 25-26, 33, 50-51, 60, 62-64, 109, 114
Heaven's Force, 31-32
Hemlock (tree), 158
Herbs, 32, 37-38, 42, 84, 109-115
Herbicide, 10, 16-17, 45
Hickory, 121, 146-148
Hiziki, 16, 158
Horseradish, 129, 134, 137, 141, 154
Horsetail, 112
Huckleberry, 118
Hybridizing, 17

Intestine, 26-27, 32, 49, 51, 127, 129-132, 136
    Large, 62-63
    Small, 62, 64
Intuition, 5, 7-9, 57, 65-66

Japanese knotweed, 37, 40, 50, 53, 91, 97
Jerky, 151
Jerusalem artichoke, 37, 99-100, 125, 133, 135, 154, 161-162, 164-166
Juneberry, 103, 118-120
Juniper, 71, 112, 114-115, 117, 168

Kale, 5, 140, 145
Kelp, 158
Ki, See also: Chi, 16-19, 21-22, 29, 31-34, 42, 57, 59, 62, 64-66, 73, 88, 111, 137, 143, 157, 165
Kidney, 4, 26-27, 61-64, 114, 126
Kinesiology, See also: Muscle testing, 74, 76
Kinnikinik, 4, 112, 114
Kombu, 16, 93, 123, 126, 132-133, 154, 158, 160

Kukicha, 113
Kushi, Michio, 31
Kuzu, 135, 150, 152

Lamb's quarter, 10, 15-16, 42, 91-92, 94-95, 100, 109, 114, 122-125, 138, 157, 159
Leaves, 25, 33, 35, 37-43, 46-47, 50-53, 55, 58, 61-62, 65, 68-69, 72-74, 77, 88-90, 92, 94-97, 99-100, 102, 105, 109, 111, 113-114, 122-123
Leek, 93, 100
Lemon balm, 91
Lentils, 160
Lettuce (wild), 87, 90-92, 94, 100, 102, 137-138
Liver, 4, 6, 26, 60-65, 89-90, 92, 94, 106, 114
Lotus, 25, 129, 133, 135, 162
Lungs, 25, 33, 60, 62-65, 129-130

Macrobiotic, 4-6, 16, 30-34, 37, 82, 111-112, 122
Mallow, 91, 94-95, 122, 124, 135, 162-164
Mammary glands, 114
Mango, 46
Maple syrup, 102, 105, 148-149
May apple, 118
Meat, 48, 50, 82, 88, 110, 117, 151
Medicine
    Oriental, 5
    Western, 5
Milk, 49, 82, 163
Milkweed, 40, 91, 94-95, 99-100, 122-123, 125
Millet, 62, 141, 143, 163
Mint, 74, 91-92, 112-116

Miso, 90, 93, 95, 100, 127, 135, 141, 145, 160-161, 166
Monoculture farming, 17
Moonseed, 151
Morel, 105-107
Mountain ash, 151
Mu tea, 153
Mugwort, 112
Mulberry, 103-104, 118-121
Mullein, 112
Muscle testing, See also: Kinesiology, 74-76
Mushroom, 3, 10, 35, 41-42, 47-48, 83, 88, 95, 105-107, 109, 127
Mustard family, 7, 16, 87, 90-91, 94, 102, 114, 117, 122, 137-138, 158-162, 164

Nettle, 4, 7, 42, 87, 91, 93-95, 99-100, 112-113, 122-125, 137-138, 145, 157, 159
Noodle, 110, 124-125, 127
Nori, 158, 161
Nut, 9, 34, 46, 48-49, 62, 83-84, 110, 117, 120-121, 129-130, 144, 146-152, 155, 162-163, 167
Nutrition, 15

Oat, 142, 145, 163
Oatmeal, 116-117, 155
Odor, 77
Ohsawa, George, 31
Onion (wild and domestic), 25, 87, 90-92, 94-96, 99, 107, 114-115, 126, 132-133, 135, 138-142, 144, 148, 160, 162-164, 166
Oranges, 5, 16

Index

Oregano, 117
Orthosympathetic nervous system, 88, 131

Pancreas, 60, 62-63, 114, 136, 150
Paracelsus, 65-66
Parasympathetic nervous system, 88, 109
Parsnip (wild and domestic), 37, 84, 99-100, 125, 130, 133-136, 142, 162-166
Pawpaw, 150-151, 153, 155
Peach, 117, 149
Peanut butter, 102
Pear, 149, 153
Pecan, 121, 147
Pemmican, 151
Peppergrass, 91, 114, 117
Peppermint, 91
Persimmon, 112, 149, 151-153, 155, 168
Pesticide, 16-17, 19, 21
Phragmites, 143
Pickles or pickling, 47-48, 50, 55, 93, 96-97, 154
Pine, 112, 158
Pineapple, 46
Pineappleweed, 112
Pitch pine, 158
Plantain, 37, 42, 87, 91-92, 100, 112, 114, 122, 137-138, 145, 157, 159
Plum (wild), 117-118, 120, 151, 153, 155
Poison ivy, 39, 41, 73-74
Poke, 137-138
Pokeweed, 16, 37-38, 41, 50, 91, 94
Potato, 37, 95
Potpourri, 112
Prostate, 136

Protein, 115, 134, 146, 148, 157
Purslane, 37, 52, 91, 122, 124, 138, 142

Radish, 125, 129
Raisin (wild and domestic), 137, 151, 153, 155
Ramp, 154
Raspberry, 112, 118, 120
Raw food, 48-49, 130
Reaction (to ingested material), 83
Redbud tree, 92, 102
Reed, 143
Rhizome, 126, 130-131, 162
Rice, 115, 123, 143
    Sweet, 62
Rice syrup, 105
Roots, 7, 9-10, 25-27, 32-35, 37, 39, 41, 46-49, 51, 55, 62, 64-65, 73-74, 83-84, 87-88, 96, 98-100, 105, 109, 125-126, 129-137, 139, 142, 148, 157, 160-166
Rose, 102, 112, 114, 117, 151
Rose hips, 4-5, 16, 41, 46, 150-151, 155, 168-169
Rutabaga, 125, 133, 145, 165-166
Rye, 99

Sage, 114
Salsify, 125-127, 133, 135, 162, 165-166
Salt, 82
Sassafras, 114, 134
Sauerkraut, 117
Scallion, 127
Seeds, 30, 33-34, 46, 48, 55, 59, 61-62, 65, 83-84, 109, 117, 120-121, 124

Sesame (oil & seeds), 16, 94-95, 97, 99, 106, 139, 148
Shape, 25, 28
Shepherd's purse, 91, 114, 117
Shibui, 43, 55
Shoots, 87, 90
Silverweed, 125, 133, 135, 142, 162, 166
Skunk cabbage, 37, 41
Soil, 17, 20-21, 44-45, 51-53, 55
Sorrel (sheep & wood), 91-92, 102, 122-124, 127, 138
Soy milk, 163
Spearmint, 91
Spices, 42, 50, 109-113, 116
Spicebush, 114
Spleen, 60, 62-63, 136, 150
Spruce, 158
Squash, 123, 125, 133, 137, 141, 144-145, 150, 163
Steiner, Rudolf, 67, 69
Stems, 7, 9, 33, 38-42, 109, 113, 152
Stomach, 26, 62, 112, 114, 127
Storage, 131
Strawberry, 41, 103-104, 112, 117-118, 121
Sugar, 49, 51, 82, 113-114
Sumac, 46, 114, 151
Sunflower, 121, 124, 134, 140, 143, 145
Survival, 15

Tahini, 95, 105, 160-161, 167
Tamari, 93-96, 99, 132-135, 139-141, 146, 154, 160-161, 164-165, 167
Taste, 35, 40, 43-44, 51-53, 55, 69, 76-77
Tea, 42, 49-50, 113-114, 117, 138, 153, 157, 159, 168

Texture, 28, 41-42, 55, 69, 77
Thistle, 42, 87-88, 90-91, 99, 114, 122, 126, 163-164
Thyme, 114
Tofu, 16, 95, 122-125, 134, 136, 161
Tomato, 95-96, 115-117
Tonic, 26, 89-90, 114
Tools, 9
Toothwort, 99, 129
Trout, 115
Tubers, 83, 98-100, 109, 125-126, 129-131, 154, 158, 161-163, 165
Turnip, 99, 125, 133, 135, 139, 145, 165-166

Umeboshi, 93
Unifying Principle, 5, 29-30, 35
Uterus, 114

Vines, 33, 55
Violet, 8, 16, 91-92, 94-95, 97, 99-100, 102, 109, 116, 122-125, 137-138, 142, 145, 157, 159
Vitamins, 19, 158
   A, 15, 26, 87, 90, 150, 157, 168
   B complex, 127, 150, 168
   C, 4-6, 16, 87, 90, 150, 157, 168
   D, 90

Wakame, 158
Walnut, 104, 120-121, 148, 152
Water hemlock, 36, 39, 44
Watercress, 3-4, 7, 16, 62, 91-92, 94-95, 106, 122, 124, 138, 140, 142, 145, 157-159, 161, 166
Wheat, 99, 136-137, 146
White pine, 158
Wild food, 82-84

Index

Wintercress, 91, 158-160
Wintergreen, 151, 168
Wright, Michele Small, 69

Yang, 30-33, 35, 37-43, 45-52, 55, 57, 61-62, 67, 69, 77, 88, 93, 100-101, 103, 105, 111, 113, 125, 129-131, 133, 139, 143, 146, 150, 152
Yang nature, 31, 37, 42, 46, 49-50
Yarrow, 70, 74, 114

Yellow nut grass, 143
Yellow pond lily, 162
Yin, 30-33, 35, 37-43, 45-53, 55, 57, 61-62, 64, 67, 69-70, 74, 77, 88, 95, 97, 101, 103, 105, 109-111, 113, 115, 117, 122, 126, 129-130, 133, 139, 142-143, 146, 150
Yin nature, 31, 41, 49
Yogurt, 49